Catherine Owen

Culture and Cooking

Or, Art in the Kitchen

Catherine Owen

Culture and Cooking
Or, Art in the Kitchen

ISBN/EAN: 9783744763776

Printed in Europe, USA, Canada, Australia, Japan

Cover: Foto ©Andreas Hilbeck / pixelio.de

More available books at **www.hansebooks.com**

CULTURE AND COOKING;

OR,

ART IN THE KITCHEN.

BY

CATHERINE OWEN.

"Le Créateur, en obligeant l'homme à manger pour vivre, l'y invite par l'appétit et l'en récompense par le plaisir."
—Brillat Savarin.

CASSELL, PETTER, GALPIN & CO.,
NEW YORK, LONDON, AND PARIS.
1881

PREFACE.

This is not a cookery book. It makes no attempt to replace a good one; it is rather an effort to fill up the gap between you and your household oracle, whether she be one of those exasperating old friends who maddened our mother with their vagueness, or the newer and better lights of our own generation, the latest and best of all being a lady as well known for her novels as for her works on domestic economy—one more proof, if proof were needed, of the truth I endeavor to set forth —if somewhat tediously forgive me—in this little book: that cooking and cultivation are by no means antagonistic. Who does not remember with affectionate admiration Charlotte Brontë taking the eyes out of the potatoes stealthily, for fear of hurting the feelings of her purblind old servant; or Margaret Fuller shelling peas?

The chief difficulty, I fancy, with women trying recipes is, that they fail and know not why they fail, and so become discouraged, and this is where I hope to step in. But although this is not a cookery book, insomuch as it does not deal chiefly with recipes, I shall yet give a few; but only when they are, or I believe them to be, better than those in general use, or good things little known, or supposed to belong to the domain of a French *chef*, of which I have introduced a good many. Should I succeed in making things that were obscure before clear to a few women, I shall be as proud as was Mme. de Genlis when she boasts in her Memoirs that she has taught six new dishes to a German housewife. Six new dishes! When Brillat-Savarin says: "He who has invented *one* new dish has done more for the pleasure of mankind than he who has discovered a star."

CONTENTS.

CHAPTER I.
PRELIMINARY REMARKS .... PAGE 1

CHAPTER II.
ON BREAD.

Sponge for bread.—One cause of failure.—Why home-made bread often has a hard crust.—On baking.—Ovens.—More reasons why bread may fail to be good.—Light rolls.—Rusks.—Kreuznach horns.—Kringles.—Brioche (Paris Jockey Club recipe).—Soufflée bread.—A novelty........ 12

CHAPTER III.
PASTRY.

Why you fail in making good puff paste.—How to succeed.—How to handle it.—To put fruit pies together so that the syrup does not boil out.—Ornamenting fruit pies.—Rissolettes.—Pastry tablets.—Frangipane tartlets.—Rules for ascertaining the heat of your oven..................... 22

CHAPTER IV.
WHAT TO HAVE IN YOUR STORE-ROOM.

Mushroom powder (recipe).—Stock to keep, or glaze (recipe).—Uses of glaze.—Glazing meats, hams, tongues, etc.—Maître d'hôtel butter (recipe).—Uses of it.—Ravigotte or Montpellier butter (recipe).—Uses of it.—Roux.—Blanc (recipes).—Uses of both.—Brown flour, its uses.......... 28

CHAPTER V.

LUNCHEONS.

Remarks on what to have for luncheons.—English meat pies.—Windsor pie.—Veal and ham pie.—Chicken pie.—Raised pork pie.—(Recipes).—Ornamenting meat pies.—Galantine (recipe).—Fish in jelly.—Jellied oysters.—A new mayonnaise luncheon for small families.—Potted meats (recipes).—Anchovy butter.—A new omelet.—Potato snow.—Lyonnaise potatoes 35

CHAPTER VI.

A CHAPTER ON GENERAL MANAGEMENT IN VERY SMALL FAMILIES.

How to have little dinners.—Hints for bills of fare, etc.—Filet de bœuf Chateaubriand (recipe).—What to do with the odds and ends.—Various recipes.—Salads.—Recipes 47

CHAPTER VII.

FRYING.

Why you fail.—Panure or bread-crumbs, to prepare.—How to prepare flounders as filets de sole.—Fried oysters.—To clarify dripping for frying.—Remarks.—Pâte à frire à la Carême.—Same, à la Provençale.—Broiling............. 55

CHAPTER VIII.

Roasting 62

CHAPTER IX.

BOILING AND SOUPS.

Boiling meat.—Rules for knowing exactly the degrees of boiling.—Vegetables.—Remarks on making soup.—To clear soup.—Why it is not clear.—Coloring pot-au-feu.—Consommé.—*Crême de celeri*, a little known soup.—Recipes.. 65

Contents. vii

CHAPTER X.

SAUCES.

Remarks on making and flavoring sauces.—Espagnole or brown sauce as it should be.—How to make fine white sauce... 70

CHAPTER XI.

WARMING OVER.

Remarks.—Salmi of cold meats.—Bœuf à la jardinière.—Bœuf au gratin.—Pseudo-beefsteak.—Cutlets à la jardinière.—Cromesquis of lamb.—Sauce piquant.—Miroton of beef.—Simple way of warming a joint.—Breakfast dish.—Stuffed beef.—Beef olives.—Chops à la poulette.—Devils.—Mephistophelian sauce.—Fritadella, twenty recipes in one... 72

CHAPTER XII.

ON FRIANDISES.

Biscuit glacée at home (recipes).—Iced soufflés (recipes).—Baba and syrups for it (recipe).—Savarin and syrup (recipes).—Bouchées de dames.—How to make Curaçoa.—Maraschino.—Noyeau... 84

CHAPTER XIII.

FRENCH CANDIES AT HOME.

How to make them.—Foudants.—Vanilla.—Almond cream.—Walnut cream.—Tutti frutti.—Various candies dipped in cream.—Chocolate creams.—Foudant panaché.—Punch drops... 91

CHAPTER XIV.

FOR PEOPLE OF VERY SMALL MEANS.

Remarks.—What may be made of a soup bone.—Several very economical dishes.—Pot roasts.—Dishes requiring no meat... 96

CHAPTER XV.

A FEW THINGS IT IS WELL TO REMEMBER.................... 105

CHAPTER XVI.

ON SOME TABLE PREJUDICES................................ 108

CHAPTER XVII.

A CHAPTER OF ODDS AND ENDS.

Altering recipes.—How to have tarragon, burnet, etc.—Remarks on obtaining ingredients not in common use.—An impromptu salamander.—Larding needle.—How to have parsley fresh all winter without expense.—On having kitchen conveniences.—Anecdote related by Jules Gouffée.—On servants in America.—A little advice by way of valedictory 111

INDEX.. 119

CULTURE AND COOKING.

CHAPTER I.

A FEW PRELIMINARY REMARKS.

ALEXANDRE DUMAS, *père*, after writing five hundred novels, says, "I wish to close my literary career with a book on cooking."

And in the hundred pages or so of preface—or perhaps overture would be the better word, since in it a group of literary men, while contributing recondite recipes, flourish trumpets in every key—to his huge volume he says, "I wish to be read by people of the world, and practiced by people of the art" (*gens de l'art*); and although *I* wish, like every one who writes, to be read by all the world, I wish to aid the practice, not of the professors of the culinary art, but those whose aspirations point to an enjoyment of the good things of life, but whose means of attaining them are limited.

There is a great deal of talk just now about cooking; in a lesser degree it takes its place as a popular topic with ceramics, modern antiques, and household art. The fact of it being in a mild way fashionable may do a little good to the eating world in general. And it may make it more easy to convince young women of refined proclivities that the art of cooking is not beneath their attention, to know that the Queen of England's daughters—and of course the cream of the London fair—have attended the lectures on the subject delivered at South Kensington, and that a young lady of rank, Sir James Coles's daughter, has been recording angel to the association, is in fact the R. C. C. who edits the "Official Handbook of Cookery."

But, notwithstanding all that has been done by South Kensington lectures in London and Miss Corson's Cooking School in New York to popularize the culinary art, one may go into a dozen houses, and find the ladies of the family with sticky fingers, scissors, and gum pot, busily porcelainizing clay jars, and not find one where they are as zealously trying to work out the problems of the "Official Handbook of Cookery."

I have nothing to say against the artistic distractions of the day. Anything that will induce love of the beautiful, and remove from us the possibility of a return to the horrors of hair-cloth and brocatel and crochet tidies, will be a stride in the right direction. But what I do protest against, is the fact, that the same refined girls and matrons, who so love to adorn their houses that they will spend hours improving a pickle jar, mediævalizing their furniture, or decorating the dinner service, will shirk everything that pertains to the preparation of food as dirty, disagreeable drudgery, and sit down to a commonplace, ill-prepared meal, served on those artistic plates, as complacently as if dainty food were not a refinement; as if heavy rolls and poor bread, burnt or greasy steak, and wilted potatoes did not smack of the shanty, just as loudly as coarse crockery or rag carpet—indeed far more so; the carpet and crockery may be due to poverty, but a dainty meal or its reverse will speak volumes for innate refinement or its lack in the woman who serves it. You see by my speaking of rag carpets and dainty meals in one breath, that I do not consider good things to be the privilege of the rich alone.

There are a great many dainty things the household of small or moderate means can have just as easily as the most wealthy. Beautiful bread—light, white, crisp, —costs no more than the tough, thick-crusted boulder, with cavities like eye-sockets, that one so frequently meets with as *home-made bread*. As Hood says:

> " Who has not met with home-made bread,
> A heavy compound of putty and lead ?"

Delicious coffee is only a matter of care, not expense— and indeed in America the cause of poor food, even in a boarding-house, is seldom in the quality of the articles so much as in the preparation and selection of them— yet an epicure can breakfast well with fine bread and butter and good coffee. And this leads me to another thing: many people think that to give too much attention to food shows gluttony. I have heard a lady say with a tone of virtuous rebuke, when the conversation turned from fashions to cooking, " I give very little time to cooking, we eat to live only "—which is exactly what an animal does. Eating to live is mere feeding. Brillat-Savarin, an abstemious eater himself, among other witty things on the same topic says, " *L'animal se repait, l'homme mange, l'homme d'esprit seul sait manger.*"

Nine people out of ten, when they call a man an epicure, mean it as a sort of reproach, a man who is averse to every-day food, one whom plain fare would fail to satisfy ; but Grimod de la Reyniere, the most celebrated gourmet of his day, author of "*Almanach des Gourmands,*" and authority on all matters culinary of the last century, said, "A true epicure can dine well on one dish, provided it is excellent of its kind." Excellent, that is it. A little care will generally secure to us the refinement of having only on the table what is excellent of its kind. If it is but potatoes and salt, let the salt be ground fine, and the potatoes white and mealy. Thackeray says, an epicure is one who never tires of brown bread and fresh butter, and in this sense every New Yorker who has his rolls from the Brevoort House, and uses Darlington butter, is an epicure. There seems to me, more mere animalism in wading through a long bill of fare, eating three or four indifferently cooked vegetables, fish, meat, poultry, each second-rate in quality, or made so by bad cooking, and declaring that you have dined well, and are easy to please, than there is in taking pains to have a perfectly broiled chop, a fine potato, and a salad, on which any true epicure could dine well, while on the former fare he would leave the table hungry.

Spenser points a moral for me when he says, speaking of the Irish in 1580, "That wherever they found a plot of shamrocks or water-cresses they had a feast;" but there were gourmets even among them, for "some gobbled the green food as it came, and some picked the faultless stalks, and looked for the bloom on the leaf."

Thus it is, when I speak of "good living," I do not mean expensive living or high living, but living so that the table may be as elegant as the dishes on which it is served.

I believe there exists a feeling, not often expressed perhaps, but prevalent among young people, that for a lady to cook with her own hands is vulgar; to love to do it shows that she is of low intellectual caliber, a sort of drawing-room Bridget. When or how this idea arose it would be difficult to say, for in the middle ages cooks were often noble; a Montmorency was *chef de cuisine* to Philip of Valois; Montesquieu descended, and was not ashamed of his descent, from the second cook of the Connetable de Bourbon, who ennobled him. And from Lord Bacon, "brightest, greatest, meanest of mankind," who took, it is said, great interest in cooking, to Talleyrand, the Machiavelli of France, who spent an hour every day with his cook, we find great men delighting in the art as a recreation.

It is surprising that such an essentially artistic people as Americans should so neglect an art which a great French writer calls the *"science mignonne* of all distinguished men of the world." Napoleon the Great so fully recognized the social value of keeping a good table that, although no gourmet himself, he wished all his chief functionaries to be so. "Keep a good table," he told them; "if you get into debt for it I will pay." And later, one of his most devoted adherents, the Marquis de Cussy, out of favor with Louis XVIII. on account of that very devotion, found his reputation as a gourmet very serviceable to him. A friend applied for a place at court for him, which Louis refused, till he heard that M. de Cussy had invented the mixture of cream, strawberries, and champagne, when he granted the petition at once. Nor is this a solitary instance in history where culinary skill has been a passport to fortune to its possessor. Savarin relates that the Chevalier d'Aubigny, exiled from France, was in London, in utter poverty, notwithstanding which, by chance, he was invited to dine at a tavern frequented by the young bucks of that day.

After he had finished his dinner, a party of young gentlemen, who had been observing him from their table, sent one of their number with many apologies and excuses to beg of him, as a son of a nation renowned for their salads, to be kind enough to mix theirs for them. He complied, and while occupied in making the salad, told them frankly his story, and did not hide his poverty. One of the gentlemen, as they parted, slipped a five-pound note into his hand, and his need of it was so great that he did not obey the prompting of his pride, but accepted it.

A few days later he was sent for to a great house, and learned on his arrival that the young gentleman he had obliged at the tavern had spoken so highly of his salad that they begged him to do the same thing again. A very handsome sum was tendered him on his departure, and afterwards he had frequent calls on his skill, until it became the fashion to have salads prepared by d'Aubigny, who became a well-known character in London, and was called "*the fashionable salad-maker.*" In a few years he amassed a large fortune by this means, and was in such request that his carriage would drive from house to house, carrying him and his various condiments —for he took with him everything that could give variety to his concoctions—from one place, where his services were needed, to another.

The contempt for this art of cooking is confined to this country, and to the lower middle classes in England. By the "lower middle classes" I mean, what Carlyle terms the gigocracy—*i.e.*, people sufficiently well-to-do to keep a gig or phaeton—well-to-do tradesmen, small professional men, the class whose womenkind would call themselves "genteel," and many absurd stories are told of the determined ignorance and pretense of these would-be ladies. But in no class above this is a knowledge of cooking a thing to be ashamed of; in England, indeed, so far from that being the case, indifference to the subject, or lack of understanding and taste for certain dishes is looked upon as a sort of proof of want of breeding. Not to like curry, macaroni, or parmesan, *paté de fois gras*, mushrooms, and such like, is a sign that you have not been all your life accustomed to good living. Mr. Hardy, in his "Pair of Blue Eyes," cleverly hits this prejudice when he makes Mr. Swancourt say, "I knew the fellow wasn't a gentleman; he had no acquired tastes, never took Worcestershire sauce."

Abroad many women of high rank and culture devote a good deal of time to a thorough understanding of the subject. We have a lady of the "lordly line of proud St. Clair" writing for us "Dainty Dishes," and doing it with a zest that shows she enjoys her work, although she does once in a while forget something she ought to have mentioned, and later still we have Miss Rose Coles writing the "Official Handbook of Cookery."

But it is in graceful, refined France that cookery is and has been, a pet art. Any bill of fare or French cookery book will betray to a thoughtful reader the attention given to the subject by the wittiest, gayest, and most beautiful women, and the greatest men. The high-sounding names attached to French standard dishes are no mere caprice or homage of a French cook to the great in the land, but actually point out their inventor. Thus *Bechamel* was invented by the Marquis de Bechamel, as a sauce for codfish; while *Filets de Lapereau à la*

Berry were invented by the Duchess de Berry, daughter of the regent Orleans, who himself invented *Pain à la d'Orleans*, while to Richelieu we are indebted for hundreds of dishes besides the renowned mayonnaise. *Cailles à la Mirepois, Chartreuse à la Mauconseil, Poulets à la Villeroy,* betray the tastes of the three great ladies whose name they bear.

But not in courts alone has the art had its devotees. Almost every great name in French literature brings to mind something its owner said or did about cooking. Dumas, who was a prince of cooks, and of whom it is related that in 1860, when living at Varennes, St. Maur, dividing his time, as usual, between cooking and literature (*Lorsqu'il ne faisait pas sauter un roman, il faisait sauter des petits oignons*), on Mountjoye, a young artist friend and neighbor, going to see him, he cooked dinner for him. Going into the poultry yard, after donning a white apron, he wrung the neck of a chicken; then to the kitchen garden for vegetables, which he peeled and washed himself; lit the fire, got butter and flour ready, put on his saucepans, then cooked, stirred, tasted, seasoned until dinner time. Then he entered in triumph and announced, "*Le diner est servi.*" For six months he passed three or four days a week cooking for Mountjoye. This novelist's book says, in connection with the fact that great cooks in France have been men of literary culture, and literary men often fine cooks, "It is not surprising that literary men have always formed the *entourage* of a great chef, for, to appreciate thoroughly all there is in the culinary art, none are so well able as men of letters; accustomed as they are to all refinements, they can appreciate better than others those of the table," thus paying himself and confrères a delicate little compliment at the expense of the non-literary world; but, notwithstanding the naïve self-glorification, he states a fact that helps to point my moral, that indifference to cooking does not indicate refinement, intellect, or social pre-eminence.

Brillat-Savarin, grave judge as he was, and abstemious eater, yet has written the book of books on the art of eating. It was he who said, "Tell me what you eat, I will tell you what you are," as pregnant with truth as the better-known proverb it paraphrases.

Malherbe loved to watch his cook at work. I think it was he who said, "A coarse-minded man could never be a cook," and Charles Baudelaire, the Poe of France, takes a poet's view of our daily wants, when he says, "that an ideal cook must have a great deal of the poet's nature, combining something of the voluptuary with the man of science learned in the chemical principles of matter;" although he goes further than we care to follow when he says, that the question of sauces and seasoning requires "a chapter as grave as a *feuilleton de science.*"

It has been said by foreigners that Americans care nothing for the refinements of the table, but I think they do care. I have known many a woman in comfortable circumstances long to have a good table, many a man aspire to better things, and if he could only get them at home would pay any money. But the getting them at home is the difficulty; on a table covered with exquisite linen, glass, and silver, whose presiding queen is more likely than not a type of the American lady—graceful, refined, and witty—on such a table, with such surroundings, will come the plentiful, coarse, commonplace dinner.

The chief reason for this is lack of knowledge on the

part of our ladies: know how to do a thing yourself, and you will get it well done by others. But how are many of them to know? The daughters of the wealthy in this country often marry struggling men, and they know less about domestic economy than ladies of the higher ranks abroad; not because English or French ladies take more part in housekeeping, but because they are at home all their lives. Ladies of the highest rank never go to a boarding or any other school, and these are the women who, with some few exceptions, know best how things should be done. They are at home listening to criticisms from papa, who is an epicure perhaps, on the shortcomings of his own table, or his neighbors'; from mamma, as to what the soup lacks, why cook is not a "*cordon bleu*," etc., while our girls are at school, far away from domestic comments, deep in the agonies of algebra perhaps; and directly they leave school, in many cases they marry. As a preparation for the state of matrimony most of them learn how to make cake and preserves, and the very excellence of their attainments in that way proves how easy it would be for them, with their dainty fingers and good taste, to far excel their European cousins in that art which a French writer says is based on "reason, health, common sense, and sound taste."

Here let me say, I do not by any means advocate a woman, who can afford to pay a first-rate cook, avoiding the expense by cooking herself; on the contrary, I think no woman is justified in doing work herself that she has the means given her to get done by employing others. I have no praise for the economical woman, who, from a desire to save, does her own work *without necessity for economy*. It is *not* her work; the moment she can afford to employ others it is the work of some less fortunate person. But in this country, it often happens that a good cook is not to be found for money, although the raw material of which one might be made is much oftener at hand. And if ladies would only practice the culinary art with as much, nay, half as much assiduity as they give to a new pattern in crochet; devote as much time to attaining perfection in one dish or article of food, be it perfect bread, or some French dish which father, brother, or husband goes to Delmonico's to enjoy, as they do to the crochet tidies or embroidered rugs with which they decorate their drawing-rooms, they could then take the material, in the shape of any ambitious girl they may meet with, and make her a fine cook. In the time they take to make a dozen tidies, they would have a dozen dishes at their fingers' ends; and let me tell you, the woman who can cook a dozen things, outside of preserves, in a *perfect* manner is a rarity here, and a good cook anywhere, for, by the time the dozen are accomplished, she will have learned so much of the art of cooking that all else will come easy. One good soup, bouillon, and you have the foundation of all others; two good sauces, white sauce and brown, "*les sauces mères*" as the French call them (mothers of all other sauces), and all others are matters of detail. Learn to make one kind of roll perfectly, as light, plump, and crisp as Delmonico's, and all varieties are at your fingers' ends; you can have kringles, Vienna rolls, Kreuznach horns, Yorkshire tea cakes, English Sally Lunns and Bath buns; all are then as easy to make as common soda biscuit. In fact, in cooking, as in many other things, "*ce n'est que le premier pas que coûte;*" failures are almost certain at the beginning, but a failure is often a step toward success—if we only know the reason of the failure.

CHAPTER II.

ON BREAD.

OF all articles of food, bread is perhaps the one about which most has been written, most instruction given, and most failures made. Yet what adds more to the elegance of a table than exquisite bread or breads, and —unless you live in a large city and depend on the baker —what so rare? A lady who is very proud of her table, and justly so, said to me quite lately, "I cannot understand how it is we never have really fine home-made bread. I have tried many recipes, following them closely, and I can't achieve anything but a commonplace loaf with a thick, hard crust; and as for rolls, they are my despair. I have wasted eggs, butter, and patience so often that I have determined to give them up, but a fine loaf I will try for."

"And when you achieve the fine loaf, you may revel in home-made rolls," I answered.

And so I advise every one first to make perfect bread, light, white, crisp, and *thin-crusted*, that rarest thing in home-made bread.

I have read over many recipes for bread, and am convinced that when the time allowed for rising is specified, it is invariably too short. One standard book directs you to leave your sponge two hours, and the bread when made up a *quarter of an hour*. This recipe strictly followed must result in heavy, tough bread. As bread is so important, and so many fail, I will give my own method from beginning to end; not that there are not numberless good recipes, but simply because they frequently need adapting to circumstances, and altering a recipe is one of the things a tyro fears to do.

I make a sponge over night, using a dried yeast-cake soaked in a pint of warm water, to which I add a spoonful of salt, and, if the weather is warm, as much soda as will lie on a dime; make this into a stiff batter with flour—it may take a quart or less, flour varies so much, to give a rule is impossible; but if, after standing, the sponge has a watery appearance, make it thicker by sprinkling in more flour, beat hard a few minutes, and cover with a cloth—in winter keep a piece of thick flannel for the purpose, as a chill is fatal to your sponge—and set in a warm place free from draughts.

The next morning, when the sponge is quite light—that is to say, at least twice the bulk it was, and like a honeycomb—take two quarts of flour, more or less, as you require, but I recommend at first a small baking, and this will make three small loaves; in winter, flour should be dried and warmed; put it in your mixing bowl, and turn the sponge into a hole in the center. Have ready some water, rather more than lukewarm, but not *hot*. Add it gradually, stirring your flour into the sponge at the same time. The great fault in making bread is getting the dough too stiff; it should be as soft as possible, without being at all sticky or wet. Now knead it with both hands from all sides into the center; keep this motion, occasionally dipping your hands into the flour if the dough sticks, but do not add more flour unless the paste sticks very much; if you have the right consistency it will be a smooth mass, very soft to the touch, *yet not sticky*, but this may not be attained at a first mixing without adding flour by degrees. When you have kneaded the dough until it leaves the bowl all round, set it in a warm place to rise. When it is well risen, feels very soft and warm to the touch, and is twice its bulk, knead it once more thoroughly, then put it in tins either floured, and the flour not adhering shaken out, or buttered, putting in each a piece of dough half the size you intend your loaf to be. Now everything depends on your oven. Many people bake their bread slowly, leaving it in the oven a long time, and this causes a thick, hard crust. When baked in the modern iron oven, quick baking is necessary. Let the oven be quite hot, then put a little ball of paste in, and if it browns palely in seven to ten minutes it is about right; if it burns, it is too hot; open the damper ten minutes. Your bread, after it is in the tins, will rise much more quickly than the first time. Let it get light, but not too light—*twice its bulk* is a good rule; but if it is light before your oven is ready, and thus in danger of getting too porous, work it down with your hand, it will not harm it, although it is better so to manage that the oven waits for the bread rather than the bread for the oven. A small loaf—and by all means make them small until you have gained experience—will not take more than three quarters of an hour to bake; when a nice yellow brown, take it out, turn it out of the tin into a cloth, and tap the bottom; if it is crisp and smells cooked, the loaf is done. Once the bottom is brown it need remain no longer. Should that, however, from fault of your oven, be not brown, but soft and white, you must put it back in the oven, the bottom upwards. An oven that does not bake at the bottom will, however, be likely to spoil your bread. It is sometimes caused by a careless servant leaving a collection of ashes underneath it; satisfy yourself that all the flues are perfectly clean and clear before beginning to bake, and if it still refuses to do its duty, change it, for you will have nothing but loss and vexation of spirit while you have it in use. I think you will find this bread white, evenly porous (not with small holes in one part and caverns in another; if it is so you have made your dough too stiff, and it is not sufficiently kneaded), and with a thin, crisp crust. Bread will surely fail to rise at all if you have scalded the yeast; the water must never be too hot. In winter, if it gets chilled, it will only rise slowly, or not at all, and in using baker's or German yeast take care that it is not stale, which will cause heavy, irregular bread.

In making bread with compressed yeast proceed in exactly the same way, excepting that the sponge will not need to be set over night, unless you want to bake very early.

If you have once produced bread to your satisfaction you will find no difficulty in making rolls. Proceed as follows:

Take a piece of the dough from your baking after it has risen once. To a piece as large as a man's fist take a large tablespoonful of butter and a little powdered sugar; work them into the dough, put it in a bowl, cover it, and set it in a warm place to rise—a shelf behind the stove is best; if you make this at the same time as your bread, you will find it takes longer to rise; the butter causes that difference; when very light, much lighter than your bread should be, take your hand and push it down till it is not larger than when you put it in the bowl; let it rise again, and again push it down, but not so thoroughly; do this once or twice more, and you have the secret of light rolls. You will find them rise very quickly, after once or twice pushing down. When they have risen the third or fourth time, take a little butter on your hands, and break off small pieces about the size of a walnut and roll them round. Either put them on a tin close together, to be broken apart, or an inch or two from each other, in which case work in a little more flour, and cut a cleft on the top, and once more set to rise; half an hour will be long enough generally, but in this case you must judge for yourself, they sometimes take an hour; if they look swelled very much and smooth they will be ready. Have a nice hot oven, and bake for twelve to fifteen minutes.

Add a little more sugar to your dough and an egg, go through the same process, brush them over with sugar dissolved in milk, and you will have delicious rusks.

The above is my own method of making rolls, and the simplest I know of; but there are numbers of other recipes given in cookery books which would be just as good if the exact directions for letting them rise were given. As a test—and every experiment you try will be so much gained in your experience—follow the recipe given for rolls in any good cookery book, take part of the dough and let it rise as therein directed, and bake, set the other part to rise as *I* direct, and notice the difference.

KREUZNACH HORNS.—Either take a third of the dough made for bread with three quarts of flour, or set a sponge with a pint of flour and a yeast-cake soaked in half a pint of warm water or milk, making it into a stiffish dough with another pint of flour; then add four ounces of butter, a *little* sugar, and two eggs; work well.

If you use the bread dough, you will need to dredge in a little more flour on account of the eggs, but not *very much;* then set to rise as for rolls, work it down twice or thrice, then turn the dough out on the molding board lightly floured, roll it as you would pie-crust into pieces six inches square, and quarter of an inch thick, make two sharp, quick cuts across it from corner to corner, and you will have from each square four three-cornered pieces of paste; spread each *thinly* with soft butter, flour lightly, and roll up very lightly from the wide side, taking care that it is not squeezed together in any way ; lay them on a tin with the side on which the point comes uppermost, and bend round in the form of a horseshoe; these will take some time to rise; when they have swollen much and look light, brush them over with white of egg (not beaten) or milk and butter, and bake in a good oven.

KRINGLES are made from the same recipe, but with another egg and two ounces of sugar (powdered) added to the dough when first set to rise; then, when well risen two or three times, instead of rolling with a pin as for horns, break off pieces, roll between your hands as thick as your finger, and form into figure eights, rings, fingers; or take three strips, flour and roll them as thick as your finger, tapering at each end ; lay them on the board, fasten the three together at one end, and then lay one over the other in a plait, fasten the other end, and set to rise, bake; when done, brush over with sugar dissolved in milk, and sprinkle with sugar.

All these breads are delicious for breakfast, and may easily be had without excessive early rising if the sponge is set in the *morning,* dough made in the afternoon, and the rising and working done in the evening ; when, instead of making up into rolls, horns, or kringles, push the dough down thoroughly, cover with a damp folded cloth, and put in a *very* cold place if in summer—not on ice of course—then next morning, as soon as the fire is alight, mold, but do not push down any more, put in a very warm spot, and when light, bake.

In summer, as I have said, I think it safest, to prevent danger of souring, to put a little soda in the sponge for bread ; and for rolls, or anything requiring to rise several times, it is an essential precaution.

BRIOCHE.—I suppose the very name of this delectable French dainty will call up in the mind's eye of many who read this book that great "little" shop, *Au Grand Brioche,* on the Boulevarde Poissonière, where, on Sunday afternoons, scores of boys from the Lycées form *en queue* with the general public, waiting the hour when the piles of golden brioche shall be ready to exchange for their eager sous. But I venture to say, a really fine brioche is rarely eaten on this side the Atlantic. They being a luxury welcome to all, and especially aromatic of Paris, I tried many times to make them, obtaining for that purpose recipes from French friends, and from standard French books, but never succeeded in producing the ideal brioche until I met with Gouffé's great book, the "*Livre de Cuisine,*" after reading which, I may here say, all secrets of the French kitchen are laid bare ; no effort is spared to make everything plain, from the humble *pot-au-feu* to the most gorgeous monumental *plât*. And I would refer any one who wants to become proficient in any French dish, to that book, feeling sure that, in following strictly the directions, there will be no failure. It is the one book I have met with on the subject in which no margin is left for your

On Bread.

own knowledge, if you have it, to fill up. But to the brioche.

PARIS JOCKEY-CLUB RECIPE FOR BRIOCHE.

Sift one pound of flour, take one fourth of it, and add rather more than half a cake of compressed yeast, dissolved in half a gill of warm water, make into a sponge with a *very little* more water, put it in a warm place; when it is double its volume take the rest of the flour, make a hole in the center, and put in it an equal quantity of salt and sugar, about a teaspoonful, and two tablespoonfuls of water to dissolve them. Three quarters of a pound of butter and four eggs, beat well, then add another egg, beat again, and add another, and so on until seven have been used; the paste must be soft, but not spread; if too firm, add another egg. Now mix this paste with the sponge thoroughly, beating until the paste leaves the sides of the bowl, then put it in a crock and cover; let it stand four hours in a warm place, then turn it out on a board, *spread it and double it four times*, return it to the crock, and let it rise again two hours; repeat the former process of doubling and spreading, and put it in a very cold place for two hours, or until you want to use it. Mold in any form you like, but the true brioche is two pieces, one as large again as the other; form the large one into a ball, make a deep depression in the center, on which place the smaller ball, pressing it gently in; cut two or three gashes round it with a sharp knife, and bake a beautiful golden brown. These brioche are such a luxury, and so sure to come out right, that the trouble of making them is well worth the taking, and for another reason: every one knows the great difficulty of making puff paste in summer, and a short paste is never handsome; but take a piece of brioche paste, roll it out thin, dredge with flour, fold and roll again, then use as you would puff paste; if for sweet pastry, a little powdered sugar may be sprinkled through it instead of dredging with flour. This makes a very handsome and delicious crust. Or, another use to which it may be put is to roll it out, cut it in rounds, lay on them mince-meat, orange marmalade, jam, or merely sprinkle with currants, chopped citron, and spices, fold, press the edges, and bake.

Before quitting the subject of breads I must introduce a novelty which I will call "soufflée bread." It is quickly made, possible even when the fire is poor, and so delicious that I know you will thank me for making you acquainted with it.

Use two or three eggs according to size you wish, and to each egg a tablespoonful of flour. Mix the yolks with the flour and with them a dessert-spoonful of butter melted, and enough milk to make a very *thick* batter, work, add a pinch of salt and a teaspoonful of sugar, work till quite smooth, then add the whites of the eggs in a firm froth, stir them in gently, and add a *quarter* teaspoonful of soda and half a one of cream of tartar. Have ready an iron frying-pan (or an earthen one that will stand heat is better), made hot with a tablespoonful of butter in it, also hot, but not so hot as for frying. Pour the batter (which should be of the consistency of sponge cake batter) into the pan, cover it with a lid or tin plate, and set it back of the stove if the fire is hot—if very slow it may be forward; when well risen and near done, put it in the oven, or if the oven is cold you may turn it gently, not to deaden it. Serve when done (try with a twig), the under side uppermost; it should be of a fine golden brown and look like an omelet. This soufflée bread is equally good *baked* in a tin in which is rather more butter than enough to grease it; the oven must be *very hot indeed*. Cover it for the few minutes with a tin plate or lid, to prevent it scorching before it has risen; when it has puffed up remove the lid, and allow it to brown, ten to fifteen minutes should bake it; turn it out as you would sponge cake—very carefully, not to deaden it. To succeed with bread you must use the very best flour.

CHAPTER III.

PASTRY.

To MAKE good puff paste is a thing many ladies are anxious to do, and in which they generally fail, and this not so much because they do not make it properly, as because they handle it badly. A lady who was very anxious to excel in pastry once asked me to allow her to watch me make paste. I did so, and explained that there was more in the manner of using than in the making up. I then gave her a piece of my paste when completed, and asked her to cover some patty pans while I covered others, cautioning her as to the way she must cover them; yet, when those covered by her came out of the oven they had not risen at all, they were like rich short paste; while my own, made from the same paste, were toppling over with lightness. I had, without saying anything, pressed my thumb slightly on one spot of one of mine; in that spot the paste had not risen at all, and I think this practical demonstration of what I had tried to explain was more useful than an hour's talk would have been.

I will first give my method of making, which is the usual French way of making "*feuilletonage.*" Take one pound of butter, or half of it lard; press all the water out by squeezing it in a cloth; this is important, as the liquid in it would wet your paste; take a third of the butter, or butter and lard, and rub it into one pound of *fine* flour; add no salt if your butter is salted; then take enough water (to which you may add the well-beaten white of an egg, but it is not absolutely necessary) to make the flour into a smooth, firm dough; it must not be too stiff, or it will be hard to roll out, or too soft, or it will never make good paste; it should roll easily, yet not stick; work it till it is very smooth, then roll it out till it is half an inch thick; now lay the whole of the butter in the center, fold one-third the paste over, then the other third; it is now folded in three, with the butter completely hidden; now turn the ends toward you, and roll it till it is half an inch thick, taking care, by rolling very evenly, that the butter is not pressed out at the other end; now you have a piece of paste about two feet long, and not half that width; flour it lightly, and fold *over* one third and under one third, which will almost bring it to a square again; turn it round so that what was the side is now the end, and roll. Most likely now the butter will begin to break through, in which case fold it, after flouring lightly, in three, as before, and put it on a dish on the ice, covering it with a damp cloth. You may now either leave it for an hour or two, or till next day. Paste made the day before it is used is much better and easier to manage, and in winter it may be kept for four or five days in a cold place, using from it as required.

When ready to use your paste finish the making by rolling it out, dredging a *little* flour, and doubling it in three as before, and roll it out thin; do this until from first to last it has been so doubled and rolled seven times.

Great cooks differ on one or two points in making pastry; for instance, Soyer directs you to put the yolk of an egg instead of the white, and a squeeze of lemon juice into the flour, and expressly forbids you to work it before adding the mass of butter, while Jules Gouffé says, "work it until smooth and shining." I cannot pretend to decide between these differing doctors, but I pursue the method I have given and always have light pastry. And now to the handling of it: It must only be touched by the lightest fingers, every cut must be made with a sharp knife, and done with one quick stroke so that the paste is not dragged at all; in covering a pie dish or patty pan, you are commonly directed to mold the paste over it as thin as possible, which conveys the idea that the paste is to be pressed over and so made thin; this would destroy the finest paste in the world; roll it thin, say for small tartlets, less than a quarter of an inch thick, for a pie a trifle thicker, then lay the dish or tin to be covered on the paste, and cut out with a knife, dipped in *hot* water or flour, a piece a little larger than the mold, then line with the piece you have cut, touching it as little as possible; press only enough to make the paste adhere to the bottom, but on no account press the border; to test the necessity of avoiding this, gently press one spot on a tart, before putting it in the oven, only so much as many people always do in making pie, and watch the result. When your tartlets or pies are made, take each up on your left hand, and with a sharp knife dipped in flour trim it round quickly. To make the cover of a pie adhere to the under crust, lay the forefinger of your right hand lengthwise round the border, but as far from the edge as you can, thus forming a groove for the syrups, and pressing the cover on at the same time. A word here about fruit pies: Pile the fruit high in the center, leaving a space all round the sides almost bare of fruit, when the cover is on press gently the paste, as I have explained, into this groove, then make two or three deep holes in the groove; the juice will boil out of these holes and run round this groove, instead of boiling out through the edges and wasting.

This is the pastry-cook's way of making pies, and makes a much handsomer one than the usual flat method, besides saving your syrup. To ornament fruit pies or tartlets, whip the white of an egg, and stir in as much powdered sugar as will make a thin meringue—a large tablespoonful is usually enough—then when your pies or tartlets are baked, take them from the oven, glaze with the egg and sugar, and return to the oven, leaving the door open; when it has set into a frosty icing they are ready to serve.

It is worth while to accomplish puff paste, for so many dainty trifles may be made with it, which, attempted with the ordinary short paste, would be unsightly. Some of these that seem to me novel I will describe.

Rissolettes are made with trimmings of puff paste; if you have about a quarter of a pound left, roll it out very thin, about as thick as a fifty-cent piece; put about half a spoonful of marmalade or jam on it, in places about an inch apart, wet lightly round each, and place a piece of paste over all; take a small round cutter as large as a dollar, and press round the part where the marmalade or jam is with the thick part of the cutter; then cut them out with a cutter a size larger, lay them on a baking tin, brush over with white of egg; then cut some little rings the size of a quarter dollar, put one on each, egg over again, and bake twenty minutes in a nice hot oven; then sift white sugar all over, put them back in the oven to glaze; a little red currant jelly in each ring looks pretty; serve in the form of a pyramid.

PASTRY TABLETS.—Cut strips of paste three inches and a half long, and an inch and a half wide, and as thick as a twenty-five cent piece; lay on half of them a thin filmy layer of jam or marmalade, not jelly; then on each lay a strip without jam, and bake in a quick oven. When the paste is well risen and brown, take them out, glaze them with white of egg and sugar, and sprinkle chopped almonds over them; return to the oven till the glazing is set and the almonds just colored; serve them hot or cold on a napkin piled log-cabin fashion.

FRANGIPANÉ TARTLETS.—One quarter pint of cream, four yolks of eggs, two ounces of flour, three macaroons, four tablespoonfuls of powdered sugar, the peel of a grated lemon, and a little citron cut very fine, a little brandy and orange-flower water. Put all the ingredients, except the eggs, in a saucepan—of course you will mix the flour smooth in the cream first—let them come to a boil slowly, stirring to prevent lumps; when the flour smells cooked, take it off the fire for a minute, then stir the beaten yolks of eggs into it. Stand the saucepan in another of boiling water and return to the stove, stirring till the eggs seem done—about five minutes, if the water boils all the time. Line patty pans with puff paste, and fill with frangipane and bake. Ornament with chopped almonds and meringue, or not, as you please.

It is very difficult to make fine puff paste in warm weather, and almost impossible without ice; for this reason I think the brioche paste preferable; but if it is necessary to have it for any purpose, you must take the following precautions:

Have your water iced; have your butter as firm as

possible by being kept on ice till the last moment; make the paste in the coolest place you have, and under the breeze of an open window, if possible; make it the day before you use it, and put it on the ice between every "turn," as each rolling out is technically called; then leave it on the ice, as you use it, taking pieces from it as you need them, so that the warmth cannot soften the whole at once, when it would become quite unmanageable. The condition of the oven is a very important matter, and I cannot do better than transcribe the rules given by Gouffé, by which you may test its fitness for any purpose:

Put half a sheet of writing paper in the oven; if it catches fire it is too hot; open the dampers and wait ten minutes, when put in another piece of paper; if it blackens it is still too hot. Ten minutes later put in a third piece; if it gets *dark brown* the oven is right for all small pastry. Called *"dark brown paper heat." Light brown paper heat* is suitable for *vol-au-vents* or fruit pies. *Dark yellow paper heat* for large pieces of pastry or meat pies, pound cake, bread, etc. *Light yellow paper heat* for sponge cake, meringues, etc.

To obtain these various degrees of heat, you try paper every ten minutes till the heat required for your purpose is attained. But remember that "light yellow" means the paper only tinged; "dark yellow," the paper the color of ordinary pine wood; "light brown" is only a shade darker, about the color of nice pie-crust, and dark brown a shade darker, by no means coffee color.

CHAPTER IV.

WHAT TO HAVE IN YOUR STORE-ROOM.

ONE great trouble with many young housekeepers is betrayed by the common remark, "Cookery books always require so many things that one never has in the house, and they coolly order you to 'moisten with gravy,' 'take a little gravy,' as if you had only to go to the pump and get it." It is very true that economy in cooking is much aided by having a supply of various condiments; warmed-over meat may then be converted into a delicious little entrée with little trouble. I would recommend, therefore, any one who is in earnest about reforming her dinner table to begin by expending a few dollars in the following articles:

1 bottle of capers,
1 " olives,
1 " gherkins,
1 " soy,
1 " anchovies,
1 " tarragon vinegar,

1 bottle of claret,
1 " white wine,
1 " sherry for cooking,
1 " brandy,
1 " Harvey sauce,
1 " walnut ketchup.

And a package of compressed vegetables and a few bay leaves.

Ten dollars thus spent may seem a good deal of money to a young housewife trying to make her husband's salary go as far as it will; but I assure her it is in the end an economy, especially in a small family, who are so apt to get tired of seeing the same thing, that it has to be thrown or given away. With these condiments and others I have yet to mention you will have no trouble in using every scrap; not using it and eating it from a sense of duty, and wishing it was something better, but enjoying it. With your store-room well provided, you can indeed go for gravy "as if to the pump."

Besides the foregoing list of articles to be bought of any good grocer, there are others which can be made at home to advantage, and once made are always ready. Mushroom powder I prefer for any use to mushroom catsup; it is easily made and its uses are infinite. Sprinkled over steak (when it must be sifted) or chops, it is delicious. For ordinary purposes, such as flavoring soup or gravy, it need not be sifted. To prepare it, take a peck of large and very fresh mushrooms, look them over carefully that they are not wormy, then cleanse them with a piece of flannel from sand or grit, then peel them and put them in the sun or a cool oven to dry; they require long, slow drying, and must become in a state to crumble. Your peck will have diminished by the process into half a pint or less of mushroom powder, but you have the means with it of making a rich gravy at a few minutes' notice.

Apropos of gravies—that much-vexed question in small households—for without gravies on hand you cannot make good hash, or many other things that are miserable without, and excellent with it. Yet how difficult it is to have gravy always on hand every mistress of a small family knows, in spite of the constant advice to "save your trimming to make stock." Do by all means save your bones, gristle, odds and ends of meat of all kinds, and convert them into broth; but even if you do, it often happens that the days you have done so no gravy is required, and then it sours quickly in summer, although it may be arrested by reboiling. In no family of three or four are there odds and ends enough, unless there is a very extravagant table kept, to insure stock for every day. My remedy for this, then, is to make a stock that will keep for months or years—in other words, *glaze*. So very rarely forming part of a housewife's stores, yet so valuable that the fact is simply astonishing; with a piece of glaze, you have a dish of soup on an emergency, rich gravy for any purpose, and all with the expenditure of less time than would make a pot of sweetmeats.

Take six pounds of a knuckle of veal or leg of beef, cut it in pieces the size of an egg, as also half a pound of lean ham; then rub a quarter of a pound of butter on the bottom of your pot, which should hold two gallons; then put in the meat with half a pint of water, three middle-sized onions, with two cloves in each, a turnip, a carrot, and a *small* head of celery; then place over a quick fire, occasionally stirring it round, until the bottom of the pot is covered with a thick glaze, which will adhere lightly to the spoon; then fill up the pot with cold water, and when on the boiling point, draw it to the back of the stove, where it may gently simmer three hours, if veal, six if beef, carefully skimming it to remove scum. This stock, as it is, will make a delicious foundation, with the addition of salt, for all kinds of clear soup or gravies. To reduce it to glaze proceed as follows: Pass the stock through a fine hair sieve or cloth into a pan; then fill up the pot again with *hot* water, and let it boil four hours longer to obtain all the glutinous part from the meat; strain, and pour both stocks in a large pot or stew-pan together; set it over the fire, and let it boil as fast as possible with the lid off, leaving a large spoon in it to prevent it boiling over, and to stir occasionally. When reduced to about three pints, pour it into a small stew-pan or saucepan, set again to boil, but more slowly, skimming it if necessary; when it is reduced to a quart, set it where it will again boil quickly, stirring it well with a wooden spoon until it begins to get thick and of a fine yellowish-brown color; at this point be careful it does not burn.

You may either pour it into a pot for use, or, what is more convenient for making gravies, get a sausage skin from your butcher, cut a yard of it, tie one end very tightly, then pour into it by means of a large funnel the glaze; from this cut slices for use. A thick slice dissolved in hot water makes a cup of nutritious soup, into which you may put any cooked vegetables, or rice, or barley. A piece is very useful to take on a journey, especially for an invalid who does not want to depend on wayside hotel food, or is tired of beef-tea.

The foregoing is the orthodox recipe for glaze, and if you have to buy meat for the purpose the very best way in which you can make it; but if it happen that you have some strong meat soup or jelly, for which you have no use while fresh, then boil it down till it is thick and brown (not burnt); it will be excellent glaze; not so fine in flavor, perhaps, but it preserves to good use what would otherwise be lost. Very many people do not know the value of pork for making jelly. If you live in the country and kill a pig, use his hocks for making glaze instead of beef.

Glaze also adds much to the beauty of many dishes. If roast beef is not quite brown enough on any one spot set your jar of glaze—for this purpose it is well to have some put in a jar as well as in the skin—in boiling water. Keep a small stiff brush; such as are sold for the purpose at house-furnishing stores, called a glazing brush, are best; but you may manage with any other or even a stiff feather. When the glaze softens, as glue would do, brush over your meat with it, it will give the lacking brown; or, if you have a ham or tongue you wish to decorate you may "varnish" it, as it were, with the melted glaze; then when cold beat some fresh butter to a white cream, and with a kitchen syringe, if you have one, a stiff paper funnel if you have not, trace any design you please on the glazed surface; this makes a very handsome dish, and if your ham has been properly boiled will be very satisfactory to the palate. Of the boiling of ham I will speak in another chapter.

I have a few more articles to recommend for your store-room, and then I think you will find yourself equal to the emergency of providing an elegant little meal if called upon unexpectedly, provided you have any cold scraps at all in the house, and *maître d'hôtel* butter.

To make the latter, take half a pound of fine butter, one tablespoonful of very fresh parsley, chopped not too fine, salt, pepper, and a small tablespoonful of lemon juice; mix together, but do not work more than sufficient for that purpose, and pack in a jar, keeping it in a cool place. A tablespoonful of this laid in a hot dish on which you serve beefsteak, chops, or any kind of fish, is a great addition, and turns plain boiled potatoes into *pomme de terre à la maître d'hôtel*. It is excellent with stewed potatoes, or added to anything for which parsley is needed, and not always at hand; a spoonful with half the quantity of flour stirred into a gill of milk or water makes the renowned *maître d'hôtel* sauce (or English parsley butter) for boiled fish, mutton, or veal. In short, it is one of the most valuable things to have in the house. Equally valuable, even, and more elegant is the preparation known as "Ravigotte" or Montpellier butter.

Take one pound in equal quantities of chervil, tarragon, burnet (pimpernel), chives, and garden cress (peppergrass); scald *two* minutes, drain quite dry; pound in a mortar three hard eggs, three anchovies, and one scant ounce of pickled cucumbers, and same quantity of capers well pressed to extract the vinegar; add salt, pepper, and a bit of garlic half as large as a pea, rub all through a sieve; then put a pound of fine butter into the mortar, which must be well cleansed from the herbs, add the herbs, with two tablespoonfuls of oil and one of tarragon vinegar, mix perfectly, and if not of a fine green, add the juice of some pounded spinach.

This is the celebrated "*beurre de Montpellier*," sold in Paris in tiny jars at a high price. Ravigotte is the same thing, only in place of the eggs, anchovies, pickles, and capers, put half a pound more butter; it is good, but less piquant.

Pack in a jar, and keep cool. This butter is excellent for many purposes. For salad, beaten with oil, vinegar, and yolks of eggs, as for mayonnaise, it makes a delicious dressing. For cold meat or fish it is excellent, and also for chops.

Two or three other articles serve to simplify the art of cooking in its especially difficult branches, and in the branches a lady finds difficult to attend to herself without remaining in the kitchen until the last minute before dinner; but with the aid of blanc and roux a fairly intelligent girl can make excellent sauces.

For roux melt slowly half a pound of butter over the fire, skim it, let it settle, then dredge in eight ounces of fine flour, stir it till it is of a bright brown, then put away in a jar for use.

Blanc is the same thing, only it is not allowed to brown; it should be stirred only enough to make all hot through, then put away in a jar.

If you need thickening for a white sauce and do not wish to stand over it yourself, having taught your cook the simple fact that a piece of blanc put into the milk *before it boils* (or it will harden instead of melt) and allowed to dissolve, stirring constantly, will make the sauce you wish, she will be able at all times to produce a white sauce that you need not be ashamed of. When the sauce is nearly ready to serve, stir in a good piece of butter—a large spoonful to half a pint; when mixed, the sauce is ready. Brown sauce can always be made by taking a cup of broth or soup and dissolving in the same way a piece of the roux; and also, if desired, a piece of Montpellier butter. If there is no soup of course you make it with a piece of glaze.

Brown flour is also a convenient thing to have ready; it is simply cooking flour in the oven until it is a *pale* brown; if it is allowed to get dark it will be bitter, and, that it may brown evenly, it requires to be laid on a large flat baking pan and stirred often. Useful for thickening stews, hash, etc.

CHAPTER V.

LUNCHEON.

LUNCHEON is usually, in this country, either a forlorn meal of cold meat or hash, or else a sort of early dinner, both of which are a mistake. If it is veritably *luncheon*, and not early dinner, it should be as unlike that later meal as possible for variety's sake, and, in any but very small families, there are so many dishes more suitable for luncheon than any other meal, that it is easy to have great variety with very little trouble.

I wish it were more the fashion here to have many of the cold dishes which are popular on the other side the Atlantic; and, in spite of the fact that table prejudices are very difficult to get over, I will append a few recipes in the hope that some lady, more progressive than prejudiced, may give them a trial, convinced that their excellence, appearance, and convenience will win them favor.

By having most dishes cold at luncheon, it makes it a distinct meal from the hot breakfast and dinner. In summer, the cold food and a salad is especially refreshing; in winter, a nice hot soup or purée—thick soup is preferable at luncheon to clear, which is well fitted to precede a heavy meal—and some savory *entrée* are very desirable, while cold raised pie, galantine, jellied fish, and potted meats may ever, at that season, find their appropriate place on the luncheon table. The potatoes, which are the only vegetable introduced at strict lunch, should be prepared in some fancy manner, as croquettes, mashed and browned, *à la maître d'hôtel*, or in snow. The latter mode is pretty and novel; I will, therefore, include it in my recipes for luncheon dishes. Omelets, too, are excellent at luncheon.

In these remarks I am thinking especially of large families, whose luncheon table might be provided with a dish of galantine, one of collared fish, and a meat pie, besides the steak, cutlets, or warmed-over meat, without anything going to waste. In winter most cold jellied articles will keep a fortnight, and in summer three or four days.

WINDSOR PIE.—Take slices of veal cutlet, half an inch thick, and very thin slices of lean boiled ham; put at the bottom of one of these veal-pie dishes or "bakers," about two to three inches deep, a layer of the veal, seasoned, then one of ham, then one of force-meat, made as follows: Take a little veal, or if you have sausage-meat ready-made, it will do, as much fine dry bread-crumbs, a dessert-spoonful of *finely* chopped parsley, in which is a salt-spoonful of powdered thyme, savory, and marjoram, if you have them, with salt and pepper, and mix with enough butter to make it a crumbling paste; lay a *thin* layer of this on the ham, then another of veal, then ham and force-meat again, until the dish is quite full. Lay something flat upon it, and then a weight for an hour. You must have prepared, from bones and scraps of veal, about a pint of stiff veal jelly; pour this over the meat, and then take strips of rich puff paste (the *brioche* paste would be excellent in hot weather), wet the edge of the dish, and lay the strips round, pressing them lightly to the dish; roll the cover a little larger than the top of the dish, and lay it on, first wetting the surface, *not the edge*, of the strips round the lips of the dish; press the two together, then make a hole in the center and ornament as you please; but I never ornament the *edge* of a pie, as it is apt to prevent the paste from rising. An appropriate and simple ornament for meat pies is to roll a piece of paste very thin, cut it in four diamond-shaped pieces, put one point of each to the hole in the center so that you have one on each end, and one each side, then roll another little piece of paste as thin as possible, flour it and double it, then double it again, bring all the corners together in your hand, like a little bundle, then with a sharp knife give a quick cut over the top of the ball of paste, cutting quite deeply, then another across; if your cut has been clean and quick, you will now be able to turn half back the leaves of paste as if it were a half-blown rose. The ends which you have gathered together in your hand are to be inserted in the hole in the center of the pie. Then brush over with yolk of egg beaten very well in a little milk or water, and bake an hour and a half.

This way of covering and ornamenting a pie is appropriate for all meat pies; pigeon pie should, however, have the little red feet skinned by dipping in boiling water, then rubbed in a cloth, when skin and nails peel off; if allowed to lie in the water, the flesh comes too; then one pair is put at each end of the pie, a hole being cut to insert them, or four are put in the center instead of the rose.

The Windsor pie is intended to be eaten cold, as are all veal and ham pies, the beauty of the jelly being lost in a hot pie. Do not fail to try it on that account, for cold pies are excellent things.

ANOTHER VEAL AND HAM PIE, more usual, and probably the "weal and hammer" that "mellered the organ" of Silas Wegg, was manufactured by Mrs. Boffin from this recipe; it is as follows:

Take the thick part of breast of veal, removing all the bones, which put on for gravy, stewing them long and slowly; put a layer of veal, pepper and salt, then a thin sprinkling of ham; if boiled, cut in slices; if raw, cut a slice in dice, which scald before using, then more veal and again ham. If force-meat balls are liked, make some force-meat as for Windsor pie, using if you prefer it chopped hard-boiled eggs in place of chopped meat, and binding into a paste with a raw egg; then make into balls, which drop into the crevices of the pie; boil two or three eggs quite hard, cut each in four and lay them round the sides and over the top, pour in about a gill of gravy, and cover the same as the Windsor pie. In either of these pies the force-meat may be left out, a sweetbread cut up, or mushrooms put in.

A chicken pie to eat cold is very fine made in this way.

RAISED PORK PIES are so familiar to every one who has visited England, and, in spite of the greasy idea, are so very good, that I introduce a well-tried recipe, feeling sure any one who eats pork at all will find it worth while to give them a trial; they will follow it with many another.

The paste for them is made as follows:

Rub into two pounds of flour a liberal half pound of butter, then melt in half a pint of hot, but not boiling milk, another half pound—or it may be lard; pour this into the flour, and knead it into a smooth, firm paste. Properly raised pies should be molded by hand, and I will endeavor to describe the method in case any persevering lady would like to try and have the orthodox thing.

But pie molds of tin, opening at the side, are to be bought, and save much trouble; the mold, if used, should be well buttered, and the pie taken out when done, and returned to the oven for the sides to brown.

To "raise" a pie, proceed thus: While the paste is warm, form a ball of paste into a cone; then with the fist work inside it, till it forms an oval cup; continue to knead till you have the walls of an even thickness, then pinch a fold all around the bottom. If properly done, you have an oval, flat-bottomed crust, with sides about two inches high; fill this with pork, fat and lean together, well peppered and salted; then work an oval cover, as near the size of the bottom cover as you can, and wet the edges of the wall, lay the cover on, and pinch to match the bottom; ornament as directed for Windsor pie, wash with egg, and bake a pale brown in a moderate oven; they must be well cooked, or the meat will not be good. One containing a pound of meat may be cooked an hour and a quarter. All these pies are served in slices, cut through to the bottom.

Galantines are very handsome dishes, not very difficult to make, and generally popular. I give a recipe for a very simple and delicious one:

Take a fine breast of veal, remove all gristle, tendons, bones, and trim to fifteen inches in length and eight wide; use the trimmings and bones to help make the jelly, then put on the meat a layer of force-meat made thus: Take one pound of sausage meat, or lean veal, to which add half a pound of bread-crumbs, parsley and thyme to taste; grate a *little* nutmeg, pepper, salt, and the juice of half a lemon; have also some long strips an inch thick of fat bacon or pork, and lean of veal, and lean ham, well seasoned with pepper, salt, and finely chopped shallots. Lay on the meat a layer of forcemeat an inch thick, leaving an inch and a half on each side uncovered; then lay on your strips of ham, veal, and bacon fat, alternately; then another of force-meat, but only half an inch thick, as too much force-meat will spoil the appearance of the dish; if you have any cold tongue, lay some strips in, also a few blanched pistachio nuts (to be obtained of a confectioner) will give the appearance of true French galantine. Roll up the veal, and sew it with a packing or coarse needle and fine twine, tie it firmly up in a piece of linen. Observe that you do not put your pistachio nuts amid the forcemeat, where, being green, their appearance would be lost; put them in crevices of the meats.

Cook this in sufficient water to cover, in which you must have the trimmings of the breast and a knuckle of veal, or hock of pork, two onions, a carrot, half a head of celery, two cloves, a blade of mace, and a good bunch of parsley, thyme and bay leaf, two ounces of salt. Set the pot on the fire till it is at boiling point, then draw it to the back and let it simmer three hours, skimming carefully; then take it from the fire, leaving it in the stock till nearly cold; then take it out, remove the string from the napkin, and roll the galantine up tighter—if too tight at first it will be hard—tying the napkin at each end only; then place it on a dish, set another dish on it, on which place a fourteen-pound weight; this will cause it to cut firm. When quite cold, remove strings and cloth, and it is ready to be ornamented with jelly. When the stock in which the galantine was cooked is cold take off the fat and clarify it, first trying, however, if it is in right condition, by putting a little on ice. If it is not stiff enough to cut firm, you must reduce it by boiling ; if too stiff, that is approaching glaze, add a *little* water, then clarify by adding whites of eggs, as directed to clarify soup (see soups). A glass of sherry and two spoonfuls of tarragon or common vinegar are a great improvement. Some people like this jelly cut in dice, to ornament the galantine, part of it may then also serve to ornament other dishes at the table. But I prefer to have the galantine enveloped in jelly, which may be done by putting it in an oblong soup tureen or other vessel that will contain it, leaving an inch space all round, then pouring the jelly over it.

Jellied fish is a favorite dish with many, and is very simple to prepare; it is also very ornamental. Take flounders or almost any flat fish that is cheapest at the time you require them. Clean and scrape them, cut them in small pieces, but do not cut off the fins; put them in a stew-pan with a few small button onions or one large one, a half teaspoonful of sugar, a glass of sherry, a dessert-spoonful of lemon juice, and a small bunch of parsley. To one large flounder put a quart of water, and if you are going to jelly oysters put in their liquor and a little salt. Stew long and slowly, skimming well; then strain, and if not perfectly clear clarify as elsewhere directed. (See if your stock jellies, by trying it on ice before you clarify.) Now take a mold, put in it pieces of cold salmon, eels that have been cooked, or oysters, the latter only just cooked enough in the stock to plump them; pour a little of the jelly in the mold, then three or four half slices of lemon, then oysters or the cold fish, until the mold is near full, disposing the lemon so that it will be near the sides and decorate the jelly; then pour the rest of the jelly over all and stand in boiling water for a few minutes, then put it in a cold place, on ice is best, for some hours. When about to serve, dip the mold in hot water, turn out on a dish, garnish with lettuce leaves or parsley and hard-boiled eggs. The latter may be introduced into the jelly cut in quarters if it is desired; very ornamental force-meat balls made bright green with spinach juice are also an improvement in appearance.

A NEW MAYONNAISE (Soyer's).—Put a quarter of a pint of stiff veal jelly (that has been nicely flavored with vegetables) on ice in a bowl, whisking it till it is a white froth; then add half a pint of salad oil and six spoonfuls of tarragon vinegar, *by degrees*, first oil, then vinegar, continually whisking till it forms a white, smooth, sauce-like cream; season with half a teaspoonful of salt, a quarter ditto of white pepper, and a very little sugar, whisk it a little more and it is ready. It should be dressed pyramidically over the article it is served with. The advantage of this sauce is that (although more delicate than any other) you may dress it to any height you like, and it will remain so any length of time; if the temperature is cool, it will remain hours without appearing greasy or melting. It is absolutely necessary, however, that it should be prepared on ice.

All these dishes, however, are only adapted for large families, but there are several ways of improving on the ordinary lunch table of very small ones. And nothing is more pleasant for the mistress of one of these very small families than to have a friend drop in to lunch, and have a *recherché* lunch to offer with little trouble. Warming over will aid her in this, and to that chapter I refer her; but there are one or two ways of having cold relishes always ready, which help out an impromptu meal wonderfully.

Potted meats are a great resource to English housekeepers; this side the Atlantic they are chiefly known through the medium of Cross & Blackwell, though latterly one or two American firms have introduced some very admirable articles of the sort. Home-made potted meats are, however, better and less expensive than those bought; they should be packed away in jars, Liebig's extract of meat jars not being too small for the purpose, as, while covered with the fat they keep well; once opened, they require eating within a week or ten days, except in very cold weather.

Potted bloater is one of the least expensive and appetizing of all potted meats. To make it, take two or three or more bloaters, cut off the heads and cleanse them, put them in the oven long enough to cook them through; take them out, take off the skin, and remove the meat from the bones carefully; put the meat of the fish in a jar with half its weight of butter, leave it to *slowly* cook in a cool oven for an hour, then take it out, put the fish into a mortar or strong dish, pour the butter on it carefully, but don't let the gravy pass too, unless the fish is to be eaten very quickly, as it would prevent it keeping. Beat both butter and fish till they form a paste, add a little cayenne, and press it into small pots, pouring on each melted butter, or mutton suet. Either should be the third of an inch thick on the bloater. This makes excellent sandwiches.

POTTED HAM.—Take any remains of ham you have, even fried, if of a nice quality, is good for the purpose; take away all stringy parts, sinew, or gristle, put it in a slow oven with its weight of butter, let it stay macerating in the butter till very tender, then beat it in a mortar, add cayenne, and pack in pots in the same way as the bloater. Thus you may pot odds and ends of any meat or fish you have, and as a little potted meat goes a long way, when you have a little lobster, a bit of chicken breast, or even cold veal, I advise you to use it in this way; you will then have a little stock of dainties in the house to fall back on at any time for unexpected calls— a very important thing in the country.

Potted chicken or veal requires either a little tongue or lean ham to give flavor; but failing these, a little ravigotte butter, beaten in after the meat is well pounded, is by no means a bad substitute.

Many people like the flavor of anchovies, but do not like the idea of eating raw fish; for these anchovy butter is very acceptable.

Take the anchovies out of the liquor in which they are packed, but do not wash them, put them in twice their weight of butter in a jar, which stand in boiling water; set all back of the stove for an hour, then pound, add cayenne, and pack in glasses.

Unexpected company to luncheon with a lady who has to eat that meal alone generally, and (as is the unwise way of such ladies) makes it a very slender meal, is one of the ordeals of a young housekeeper; company to lunch and nothing in the house. But there is generally a dainty luncheon in every house if you know how to prepare it; there certainly always will be if you keep your store-room supplied with the things I have named. Let the table be prettily laid at all times, then if you have potted meat and preserves, have them put on the table. Are there cold potatoes? If so cut them up into potato salad, if they are whole; if broken, warm them in a wine-glass of milk, a teaspoonful of flour, and a piece as large as an egg of *maître d'hôtel* butter. Have you such scraps of cold meat as could not come to table? Toss them up with a half cup of water, a slice of glaze (oh, blessed ever-ready glaze!) a teaspoonful of ravigotte, or *maitre d'hôtel*, and a teaspoonful of roux or blanc, according as your meat is light or dark, season, and serve. Or you have no meat, then you have eggs, and what better than an omelet and such an omelet as the following? Take the crumb of a slice of bread, soak it in hot milk (cold will do, but hot is better), beat up whites of four eggs to a high froth; mix the bread with all the milk it will absorb, *no more*, into a paste, add the yolks of eggs with a little salt, set the pan on the fire with an ounce of butter. Let it get very hot, then mix the whites of eggs with the yolks and bread lightly, pour in the pan, and move about for a minute; if the oven is hot, when the omelet is brown underneath, set the pan in the oven for five minutes, or until the top is set; then double half over, and serve. If your guests have a liking for sweets, and your potted meats supply the savory part of your luncheon, then have a brown gravy ready to serve with it. Put into a half cup of boiling water a slice of glaze, a spoonful of roux, and enough Harvey sauce, or mushroom powder, to flavor. If your omelet is to be sweet, before you fold it put in a layer of preserves.

The advantage of the omelet I have here given is that it keeps plump and tender till cold, so that five minutes of waiting does not turn it into leather, the great objection with omelets generally.

Potatoes for luncheon, as I have said, should always be prepared in some fancy way, and snow is a very pretty one. Have some fine mealy potatoes boiled, carefully poured off, and set back of the stove with a cloth over them till they are quite dry and fall apart; then have a colander, or coarse wire sieve made *hot* and a *hot* dish in which .to serve them, pass the floury potatoes through the sieve, taking care not to crush the snow as it falls. You require a large dish heaping full. and be careful it is kept hot.

This mode of preparing potatoes, although very pretty and novel, must never be attempted with any but the whitest and mealiest kind.

The remains of cold potatoes may be prepared thus: Put three ounces of butter in a frying-pan in which fry three onions sliced till tender, but not very brown, then put on the potatoes cut in slices, and shake them till they are of a nice brown color, put a spoonful of chopped parsley, salt, pepper, and juice of a lemon, shake well that all may mix together, dish, and serve very hot.

CHAPTER VI.

A CHAPTER ON GENERAL MANAGEMENT IN VERY SMALL FAMILIES.

A VERY small family, "a young *ménage*," for instance, is very much more difficult to cater for without waste than a larger one; two people are so apt to get tired of anything, be it ever so good eating, when it has been on the table once or twice; therefore it would be useless to make galantine or the large pies I have indicated, except for occasions when guests are expected; but, as I hope to aid young housekeepers to have nice dishes when alone, I will devote this chapter to their needs.

The chapter on "Warming Over" will be very useful also to this large class.

In the first place it is well to have regard, when part of a dish leaves the table, as to whether it, or any particular part of it, will make a nice little cold dish, or a *rechauffé*; in that case have it saved, unless it is required for the servants' dinner (it is well to manage so that it is not needed for that purpose); for instance, if there is the wing and a slice or two of the breast of a chicken left, it will make a dainty little breakfast dish, or cold, in jelly, be nice for lunch. There is always jelly if you have roast chicken, if you manage properly, and this is how you do it:

Carefully save the feet, throat, gizzard, and liver of your chickens; scald the feet by pouring boiling water over them; leave them just a minute, and pull off the outer skin and nails; they come away very readily, leaving the feet delicately white; put these with the other giblets, properly cleansed, into a small saucepan with an onion, a slice of carrot, a sprig of parsley, and a pint of water (if you have the giblets of one chicken), if of two, put a quart; let this *slowly* simmer for two hours and a half; it will be reduced to about half, and form a stiff jelly when cold; a glass of sherry, and squeeze of lemon, or teaspoonful of tarragon vinegar, makes this into a delicious aspic, and should be added if to be eaten cold. The jelly must of course be strained.

In roasting chickens, if you follow the rule for meat, that is, put no water in the pan, but a piece of butter, and dredge a *very little* flour over the chicken, you will have a nice brown glaze at the bottom of the pan, provided it has been cooked in a *quick oven;* if in a cool oven there will be nothing brown at all; but we will suppose the bird is browned to a turn; pour your gravy from the giblets into the pan, take off every bit of the glaze or osmazone that adheres, and let it dissolve, rubbing it with the back of the spoon; then, if you are likely to have any chicken left cold, pour off a little gravy in a cup through a fine strainer, leaving in your pan sufficient for the dinner; in this mash up the liver till it is a smooth paste which thickens the gravy, and serve. Some object to liver, therefore the use of it is a matter of taste. If you dress the chickens English fashion, you will *need* the liver and gizzard to tuck under the wings; in this case, stew only the feet and throat, using a little meat of any kind, if you have it, to take their place; but on no account fail to use the feet, as they are as rich in jelly as calves' feet in proportion to their size.

The jelly laid aside will be enough to ornament and give relish to a little dish of cold chicken, and changes it from a dry and commonplace thing to a *recherché* one. If two chickens are cooked it is more economical than one; there is, then, double the amount of gravy, generally sufficient, if you lay some very nice pieces of cold chicken in a bowl, to pour over it and leave it enveloped in jelly; you still then, if from dinner for two people, have perhaps joints enough to make a dish of curry or fricassee, or any of the many ways in which cold chicken may be used, for which see chapter on "*Warming Over.*"

For small households large joints are to be avoided, but even a small roast is a large joint when there are but two or three to eat it. For this reason it is a good plan to buy such joints as divide well. A sirloin of beef is better made into two fine dishes than into one roast, and then warmed over twice. Every one knows that "*Filet de bœuf Chateaubriand*" is one of the classical dishes of the French table, that to a Frenchman luxury can go no further; but every one does not know how entirely within his power it is to have that dish as often as he has roast beef; how convenient it would be to so have it. Here it is: When your sirloin roast comes from the butcher, take out the tenderloin or fillets, which you must always choose thick; cut it across into steaks an inch thick, trim them, cover them with a coat of butter (or oil, which is much better), and broil them ten minutes, turning them often; garnish with fried potatoes, and serve with *sauce Chateaubriand*, as follows: Put a gill of white wine (or claret will do if you have no white) into a saucepan, with a piece of glaze, weighing an ounce and a half; add three quarters of a pint of *espagnole*, and simmer fifteen minutes; when ready to serve, thicken with two ounces of *maître d'hôtel* butter in which a dessert-spoonful of flour has been worked. That is how Jules Gouffé's recipe runs; but, as no small family will keep *espagnole* ready made, allow a little more glaze (of course the recipe as given may be divided to half or quarter, provided the correct proportions are retained), and use a tablespoonful of roux and the *maître d'hôtel* butter, both of which you have probably in your store-room; if not, brown a little flour, chop some parsley, and add to two ounces of butter; work them together, then let them dissolve in the sauce, for which purpose let it go off the boil; let the sauce simmer a minute, skim, and serve.

The sirloin of beef, denuded of its fillet, is still a good roast; and as you can't have your cake and eat it too, and hot fresh roast beef is better than the same warmed over, warm ye never so wisely, I think this plan may commend itself to those who like nice *little* dinners.

A nice little dinner of a soup, an *entrée*, or made dish, salad, and dessert, really costs no more than frequent roast meat, or even steak and pudding, by following some such plan as this:

Sunday.—*Pot-au-feu* and roast lamb, leg of mutton or other good joint, etc.

Monday.—Rice or vermicelli soup made with remains of the *bouillon* from *pot-au-feu*. If the Sunday joint was a fore or hindquarter of lamb it should have been divided, say the leg from the loin, thus providing choice roasts for two days, and yet having enough cold lamb—that favorite dish with so many—for luncheon with a salad; and, surprising to say, after hot roast lamb for dinner Sunday, cold lunch for Monday, another roast Monday, and cold or warmed up for lunch Tuesday, there will still be (supposing as I do, in preparing this chapter, that the family consists only of gentleman, lady, and servant) remains enough from the two cold joints to make cromesquis of lamb (see recipe), a little dish of mince, or a delicate *sauté* of lamb for breakfast. It is surprising what may be done with odds and ends in a small family; a tiny plate of pieces, far too small to make an appearance on the table, and which, if special directions are not given, will seem to Bridget not worth saving, will, with each piece dipped into the batter *à la Carême*, and fried in hot fat, make a tempting dish for breakfast, or an *entrée* for dinner or luncheon. Two tablespoonfuls only of chopped meat of any kind will make croquettes for two or three people; hence, 'save the pieces.' But to return to our bills of fare : I have given the two roasts of lamb for consecutive days, because the weather in lamb season is usually too warm to keep it; when this can be done, however, it is pleasanter to leave the second joint of lamb till Tuesday. Should a forequarter (abroad held in greater esteem than the hindquarter) have been chosen, get the butcher to take out the shoulder in one round thick joint, English fashion; this crisply roasted is far more delicious than the leg; you then have the chops to be breaded, and an excellent dish of the neck and breast, either broiled, curried, stewed with peas, or roast.

Yet how often we see a whole quarter of lamb put in the oven for two or three people who get tired of the sight of it cold, yet feel in economy bound to eat it.

Should sirloin of beef have been the Sunday dinner, you will know what to do with it, from directions already given; and as a sirloin of beef, even with the fillet out, will be more than required for one dinner, it may serve for a third day, dressed in one of the various ways I shall give in chapter on "Warming Over." You have still at your disposal the bouilli or beef from which you have made your *pot-au-feu*, which, if it has been carefully boiled, not galloped, nor allowed to fall to rags, is very good eating. Cut thin with lettuce, or in winter celery, in about equal quantities, and a good salad dressing, it is excellent; or, made into hash, fritadella, or even rissoles, is savory and delicious; only bear in mind with this, as all cooked meats, the gravy drawn out must be replaced by stock or glaze; it is very easy to warm over bouilli satisfactorily, as a cup of the soup made from it can always be kept for gravy.

A leg of mutton makes two excellent joints, and is seldom liked cold—as beef and lamb often are.

Select a large fine leg, have it cut across, that each part may weigh about equally; roast the thick or fillet end and serve with or without onion sauce (*à la soubise*); boil the knuckle in a small quantity of water, just enough to cover it, with a carrot, turnip, onion, and bunch of parsley, and salt in the water, serve with caper sauce and mashed turnips. The broth from this is excellent soup served thus: Skim it carefully, take out the vegetables, and chop a small quantity of parsley very fine, then beat up in a bowl two eggs, pour into them a little of the broth—not boiling—beating all the time, then draw your soup back till it is off the boil, and pour in the eggs, stirring continually till it is on the boiling point again (but it must not boil, or the eggs will curdle and spoil the soup), and then turn it into a *hot* tureen and serve. Use remains of the cold roast and boiled mutton together, to make made dishes; between the days of having the roast and boiled mutton you may have had a fowl, and the remains from that will make you a second dish to go with your joint.

The remains from the first cooked mutton, in form of curry, mince, salmi, or *sauté*, will be a second dish with your fowl.

Veal is one of the most convenient things to have for a small family, as it warms over in a variety of ways, and in some is actually better than when put on the table as a joint. By having a little fish one day, instead of soup, and a little game another, and remembering when you have an especially dainty thing, to have one with it a little more substantial and less costly, you may have variety at little expense.

For instance, if you find it convenient to have for dinner fritadelle (see " *Warming Over*") or miroton of beef, or cold mutton curried, you might have broiled birds, or roast pigeon, or game. In this consists good management, to live so that the expenses of one day balance those of the other—unless you are so happily situated that expense is a small matter, in which case these remarks will not apply to you at all. Then, never mind warming over, or making one joint into two; let your poor neighbors and Bridget's friends enjoy your superfluity. To the woman with a moderate income it usually is a matter of importance, or ought to be, that her weekly expenditure should not exceed a certain amount, and for this she must arrange that any extra expense is balanced by a subsequent economy.

Salads add much to the health and elegance of a dinner; it is in early spring an expensive item if lettuce is used; but no salad can be more delicious or more healthful than dressed celery; and by buying when cheap, arranging with a man to lay in your cellar, covered with soil, enough for the winter's use, it need cost but moderately. Celeraic, or turnip-rooted celery is another salad that is very popular with our German friends; it is a bulbous celery, the root being the part eaten; these are cooked like potatoes, cut in slices, and dressed with oil and vinegar, or mayonnaise, it is exceedingly good. Potato salad is always procurable, and in summer at lunch, instead of the hot vegetable, or in winter when green salad is dear, is very valuable. It may be varied by the addition, one day, of a few chopped pickles, another, a little onion, or celery, or parsley, or tarragon, a little ravigotte butter beaten to cream with the vinegar, or with meat, as follows: Boil the potatoes in their skins, peel them, cut them into pieces twice the thickness of a fifty-cent piece, and put them into a salad bowl with cold meat (bouilli from soup is excellent); put to them a teaspoonful of salt, half that quantity of pepper, two tablespoonfuls of vinegar, three or even four of oil, and a teaspoonful of chopped parsley. You can vary this by putting at different times some chopped celery or pickles, olives, or anchovies.

CHAPTER VII.

ON FRYING AND BROILING.

FRYING is one of the operations in cookery in which there are more failures than any other, or, at least, there appear to be more, because the failure is always so very apparent. Nothing can make a dish of breaded cutlets on which are bald white spots look inviting, or lividlooking fish, just flaked here and there with the bread that has been persuaded to stay on. And, provided you have enough fat in the pan—there should always be enough to immerse the article; therefore use a deep iron or enameled pan—there can be but two reasons why you fail. Your fat has not been hot enough, or your crumbs have not been fine and *even*.

Many suppose when the fat bubbles and boils in the pan that it is quite hot; it is far from being so. Others again are so much nearer the truth that they know it must become *silent*, that is, boil and cease to boil, before it is ready, but even that is not enough; it must be silent some time, smoke, and appear to be on the point of burning, then drop a bit of bread in; if it crisps and takes color directly, quickly put in your articles.

These articles, whether cutlets or fish, must have been carefully prepared, or herein may lie the second cause of failure. Any cookery book will give you directions how to crumb, follow them; but what some do not tell you is, that your bread-crumbs should be *finely sifted;* every coarse crumb is liable to drop off and bring with it a good deal of the surrounding surface.

I also follow the French plan in using the egg, and mix with it oil and water in the proportion of three eggs, one tablespoonful of oil, one of water, and a little salt, beat together and use. It is a good plan to keep a supply of *panure* or dried bread-crumbs always ready. Cut any slices of baker's bread, dry them in a cool oven so that they remain quite colorless, or they will not do for the purpose. When as dry as crackers, crush under a rolling-pin, and sift; keep in a jar for use.

In no branch of cooking is excellence more appreciated than in that of frying. A dish of *filets de sole* or cutlets, crisp and golden brown, is an ornament to any table, and is seldom disdained by any one. Apropos of *filets de sole;* it is very high-sounding yet very attainable, as I shall show. I was staying with a friend early in spring, a lady always anxious for table novelties. "Oh, do tell me what fish to order, I should like something fried, now that you are here to tell cook how to do it; she hasn't the wildest idea, although she would be astounded to hear me say so." "Have you ever had flounders?" I asked. "Flounders!" My friend's pretty nose went up the eighth of an inch, and her confidence in my powers as counselor went down to zero. "Flounders! but they are a very common fish you know." "I know they are very delicious," I answered. "Order them, and trust me; but I must coax the autocrat of your kitchen to allow me to cook and prepare them myself."

An hour before dinner I went into the kitchen, put at least a pound of lard into a deep frying-pan, and set it where it would get gradually hot, then I turned my attention to the fish ; they were thick, firm flounders, and were ready cleaned, scraped, and the heads off. I then proceeded to bone one in the following way : Take a sharp knife and split the flounder right down the middle of the back, then run the knife carefully between the flesh and bones going toward the edge. You have now detached one quarter of the flesh from the bone, do the other half in the same way, and when the back is thus entirely loose from the bone, turn the fish over and do the same with the other part. You will now find you can remove the bone whole from the fish, detaching, as you do so, any flesh still retaining the bone, then you have two halves of the fish ; cut away the fins, and you have four quarters of solid fish. Now see if the fat is very hot, set it forward while you wipe your fish dry, and dip each piece in milk, then in flour. Try if the fat is hot by dropping a crumb into it; if it browns at once, put in the fish. When they are beautifully brown, which will be in about ten minutes, take them up in the colander, and then lay them on a towel to absorb any fat, lay them on a hot dish, and garnish with slices of lemon and parsley or celery tops.

Now when this dish made its appearance, my friend's husband, a *bon vivant*, greeted it with, "Aha ! *Filets de sole à la Delmonico*," and as nothing to the contrary was said until dinner was over, he ate them under the impression that they were veritable *filets de sole*. Of course I can't pretend to say whether M. Delmonico imports his soles, or uses the homely flounder ; but I do know that one of his frequenters knew no difference.

Oysters should be laid on a cloth to drain thoroughly, then rolled in fine sifted cracker dust, and dropped into very hot fat; do not put more oysters in the pan than will fry without one overlapping the other. Very few minutes will brown them beautifully, if your fat was hot enough, and as a minute too long toughens and shrinks them, be very careful that it browns a cube of bread almost directly, before you begin the oysters. Egg and bread-crumb may be used instead of cracker dust, but it is not the proper thing, and is a great deal more trouble. Should you be desirous of using it, however, the oysters must be carefully wiped *dry* before dipping them; while for cracker dust they are not wiped, but only drained well.

Fish of any kind, fried in batter *à la Carême* (see recipe), is very easy to do, and very nice.

Carefully save veal, lamb, beef, and pork drippings. Keep a crock to put it in, and, clarified as I shall direct, it is much better than lard for many purposes, and for frying especially; it does not leave the dark look that is sometimes seen on articles fried in lard. The perfection of "friture," or frying-fat, according to Gouffé, is equal parts of lard and beef fat melted together.

Yet there are families where dripping is never used— is looked upon as unfit to use—while the truth is that many persons quite unable to eat articles fried in lard would find no inconvenience from those fried in beef fat. It is as wholesome as butter, and far better for the purpose. Butter, indeed, is only good for frying such things as omelets or scrambled eggs; things that are cooked in a very short time, and require no great degree of heat.

The same may be said of oil, than which, for fish, nothing can be better. Yet it can only be used once, and is unsuitable for things requiring long-sustained heat, as it soon gets bitter and rank.

Do not be afraid to put a pound or two of fat in your pan for frying; it is quite as economical as to put less for it can be used over and over again, a pail or crock being kept for the purpose of receiving it. Always in returning it to the crock pour it through a fine strainer, so that no sediment or brown particles may pass which would spoil the next frying.

To clarify dripping, when poured from the meat-pan, it should go into a bowl, instead of the crock in which you wish to keep it. Then pour into the bowl also some boiling water, and add a little salt, stir it, and set it away. Next day, or when cold, run a knife round the bowl, and (unless it is pork) it will turn out in a solid cake, leaving the water and impurities at the bottom. Now scrape the bottom of your dripping, and put it in more boiling water till it melts, then stir again, another pinch of salt add, and let it cool again. When you take off the cake of fat, scrape it as before, and it is ready to be melted into the general crock, and will now keep for months in cool weather. If you are having frequent joints it is as well to do all your dripping together, once a week; but do not leave it long at any season with water under it, as that would taint it. Fat skimmed from boiled meat, *pot-au-feu*, before the vegetables, etc., go in, is quite as good as that from roast, treated in the same way.

Frying in batter is very easy and excellent for some things, such as warming over meat, being far better than eggs and crumbs. Carême gives the following recipe, which is excellent:

Three quarters of a pound of sifted flour, mixed with two ounces of butter melted in warm water; blow the butter off the water into the flour first, then enough of the water to make a *soft* paste, which beat smooth, then more warm water till it is batter thick enough to mask the back of a spoon dipped into it, and salt to taste; add the *last thing* the whites of two eggs well beaten.

Another batter, called *à la Provençale*, is also exceedingly good, especially for articles a little dry in themselves, such as chickens to be warmed over, slices of cold veal, etc.

Take same quantity of flour, two yolks of eggs, four tablespoonfuls of oil, mix with *cold* water, and add whites of eggs and salt as before. Into this batter I sometimes put a little chopped parsley, and the least bit of powdered thýme, or grated lemon-peel, or nutmeg; this is, however, only a matter of taste.

BROILING is the simplest of all forms of cooking, and is essentially English. To broil well is very easy with a little attention. A brisk clear fire, not too high in the stove, is necessary to do it with ease; yet if, as must sometimes happen, to meet the necessities of other cooking, your fire is very large, carefully fix the gridiron on two bricks or in any convenient manner, to prevent the meat scorching, then have the gridiron *very hot* before putting your meat upon it; turn it, if chop or steak, as soon as the gravy begins to start on the upper side; if allowed to remain without turning long, the gravy forms a pool on the top, which, when turned, falls into the fire and is lost; the action of the heat, if turned quickly, seals the pores and the gravy remains in the meat. If the fire is not very clear, put a cover over the meat on the gridiron, it will prevent its blackening or burning—if the article is thick I always do so—and it is an especially good plan with birds or chickens, which are apt to be raw at the joints unless this is done; indeed, with the latter, I think it a good way to put them in a hot oven ten minutes before they go on to broil, then have a spoonful of *máitre d'hôtel* butter to lay on the breast of each. Young spring chickens are sometimes very dry, in which case dip them in melted butter, or, better still, oil them all over a little while before cooking. There is nothing more unsightly than a sprawling dish of broiled chickens; therefore, in preparing them place them in good form, then, with a gentle blow of the rolling-pin, break the bones that they may remain so.

CHAPTER VIII.

ROASTING.

In spite of Brillat-Savarin's maxim that one may become a cook, but must be born a *rotisseur*, I am inclined to think one may also, by remembering one or two things, become a very good "roaster" (to translate the untranslatable), especially in our day, when the oven has taken the place of the spit, although a great deal of meat is spoiled in roasting ; a loin of lamb or piece of beef, that comes to the table so pale that you can't tell whether it has been boiled or merely wilted in the oven, is an aggravation so familiar, that a rich brown, well-roasted joint is generally a surprise. Perhaps the cook will tell you she has had the "hottest kind of an oven;" but then she has probably also had a well of water underneath it, the vapor from which, arising all the time, has effectually soddened the meat, and checked the browning. The surface of roast meat should be covered with a rich glaze, scientifically called "osmazone." That the meat may be thus glazed, it should always go into a *hot* oven, so that, as the gravy exudes, it may congeal on the outside, thus sealing up the pores. The general plan, however, is to put meat into a warm oven an hour or two earlier than it should go, with a quantity of water and flour underneath it. The result in hot weather I have known to be very disagreeable, the tepid oven having, in fact, given a stale taste to the joint

Roasting. 63

before it began to cook, and it at all times results in flavorless, tough meat. There is no time saved, either, in putting the meat in while the oven is yet cool. Heat up the oven till it is quite brisk, then put the meat in a pan, in which, if it is fat, you require *no water;* if very lean, you may put half a teacup, just enough to prevent the pan burning; you may rub a little flour over the joint or not, as you please, but never more than the surface moisture absorbs; have no clinging particles of flour upon the joint, neither put salt nor pepper upon the meat before it goes into the oven; salt draws out the gravy, which it is your object to keep in, and the flavor of pepper is entirely changed by the parching it undergoes when on the surface of the meat, the odor of scorched pepper, while cooking, being very offensive to refined nostrils. This does not occur when pepper is not on the surface; for the *inside* of birds, in stuffing, and in meat pies it is indispensable, and the flavor undergoes no change. This remark on pepper applies also to broiling and frying. Always pepper *after* the article is cooked, and both for appearance and delicacy of flavor white pepper should always be used in preference to black.

Meat, while in the oven, should be carefully turned about so that it may brown equally, and when it has been in half the time you intend to give it, or when the upper surface is well browned, turn it over. When it comes out of the oven put it on a hot dish, then carefully pour off the fat by holding the corner of the meat pan over your dripping-pan, and very gently allowing the fat to run off; do not shake it; when you see the thick brown sediment beginning to run too, check it; if there is still much fat on the surface, take it off with a spoon; then pour into the pan a little boiling water and salt, in quantity according to the quantity of sediment or glaze in the pan, and with a spoon rub off every speck of the dried gravy on the bottom and sides of the pan. Add no flour, the gravy must be thick enough with its own richness. If you have added too much water, so that it looks poor, you may always boil it down by setting the pan on the stove for a few minutes; but it is better to put very little water at first, and add as the richness of the gravy allows. Now you have a rich brown gravy, instead of the thick whitey-brown broth so often served with roast meat. Every drop of this gravy and that from the dish should be carefully saved if left over.

Save all dripping, except from mutton or meat with which onions are cooked, for purposes which I shall indicate in another place.

Veal and pork require to be very thoroughly cooked. For them, therefore, the oven must not be too hot, neither must it be lukewarm, a good even heat is best; if likely to get too brown before it is thoroughly cooked, open the oven door.

CHAPTER IX.

BOILING.

BOILING is one of the things about which cooks are most careless; theoretically they almost always know meat should be slowly boiled, but their idea of "slow" is ruled by the fire; they never attempt to rule that. There is a good rule given by Gouffé as to what slow boiling actually is: the surface of the pot should only show signs of ebullition at one side, just an occasional bubble. *Simmering* is a still slower process, and in this the pot should have only a sizzling round one part of the edge. All fresh meat should boil *slowly;* ham or corn beef should barely simmer. Yet they must not go off the boil at all, which would spoil fresh meat entirely; steeping in water gives a flat, insipid taste.

All vegetables except potatoes, asparagus, peas, and cauliflower should boil as fast as possible; these four only moderately. Most vegetables are boiled far too long. Cabbage is as delicate as cauliflower in the summer and fall if boiled in plenty of water, to which a salt spoonful of soda has been added, as *fast as possible* for twenty minutes or half an hour, then drained and dressed. In winter it should be cut in six or eight pieces, boiled *fast*, in plenty of water, for half an hour, *no longer*. Always give it plenty of room, let the water boil rapidly when you put it in the pot, which set on the hottest part of the fire to come to that point again, and you will have no more strong, rank, yellow stuff on your table, no bad odor in your house. Peas require no more than twenty minutes' boiling if young; asparagus the same; the latter should always be boiled in a saucepan deep enough to let it stand up in the water when tied up in bunches, for this saves the heads. Potatoes should be poured off the minute they are done, and allowed to stand at the back of the stove with a clean cloth folded over them. They are the only vegetable that should be put into *cold* water. When new, boiling water is proper. When quite ripe they are more floury if put in cold water.

Soups.—As I have before said, I do not pretend to give many recipes, only to tell you how to succeed with the recipes given in other books. I shall, therefore, only give one recipe which I know is a novelty and one for the foundation of all soups. In one sense I have done the latter already. The stock for glaze is an excellent soup before it is reduced; but I will also give Jules Gouffé's method of making *pot-au-feu*, it being a most beautifully clear soup.

It often happens, however, that you have sufficient stock from bones, trimmings of meat, and odds and ends of gravies, which may always be turned to account; but the stock from such a source, although excellent, will not always be clear; therefore, you must proceed with it in the following manner, unless you wish to use it for thick soup:

Make your stock boiling hot and skim well; then have ready the whites of three eggs (I am supposing you have three quarts of stock—one egg to a quart), to which add half a pint of cold water; whisk well together; then add half a pint of the boiling stock gradually, still whisking the eggs; then stir the boiling stock rapidly, pouring in the whites of eggs, etc.; as you do it, stir quickly till nearly boiling again, then take it from the fire, let it remain till the whites of eggs separate; then strain through a clean, fine cloth into a basin. This rule once learned will clear every kind of soup or jelly.

There are many people who are good cooks, yet fail in clear soup, which is with them semi-opaque, while it should be like sherry. The cause of this opacity is generally quick boiling while the meat is in. This gives it a milky appearance. After the stock is once made and clear, quick boiling will do no harm, but of course wastes the soup, unless resorted to for the purpose of making it stronger. A word here about coloring soup: Most persons resort to burnt sugar, and, very carefully used, it is not at all a bad makeshift. But how often have we a rich-looking soup put before us, the vermicelli appearing to repose under a lake of strong russet *bouillon*, but which, on tasting, we find suggestive of nothing but burnt sugar and salt, every bit of flavor destroyed by the acrid coloring. Sometimes stock made by the recipe for *pot-au-feu* (to follow) requires no color; this depends on the beef; but usually all soup is more appetizing in appearance for a little browning, and for this purpose I always use burnt onions in preference to anything else. If you have none in store when the soup is put on, put a small onion in the oven (or on the back of the stove; should you be baking anything the odor would taint); turn it often till it gets quite black, but not *charred*. Then put it to the soup; it adds a fine flavor as well as color, and you need not fear overdoing it.

Soup that is to be reduced must be very lightly salted; for this reason salt is left out altogether for glaze, as the reduction causes the water only to evaporate, the salt remains.

GOUFFÉ'S POT-AU-FEU.—Four pounds of lean beef, six quarts of water, six ounces of carrot, six of turnip, six of onion, half an ounce of celery, one clove, salt.

Put the meat on in cold water, and just before it comes to the boil skim it, and throw in a wineglass of cold water, skim again, and, when it is "on the boil," again throw in another wineglass of cold water; do this two or three times. The object of adding the cold water is to keep it just off the boil until all the scum has risen, as the boiling point is when it comes to the surface, yet once having boiled, the scum is broken up, and the soup is never so clear.

The meat must simmer slowly, *not boil*, for three hours before the vegetables are added, then for a couple of hours more.

It is necessary to be very exact in the proportions of vegetables; but, of course, after having weighed them for soups once or twice, you will get to know about the size of a carrot, turnip, etc., that will weigh six ounces. The exact weight is given until the eye is accustomed to it.

This soup strained, and boiled down to one half, becomes *consommé*.

CELERY CREAM is a most delicious and little-known white soup, and all lovers of good things will thank me for introducing it.

Have some nice veal stock, or the water in which chickens have been boiled, reduced till it is rich enough, will do, or some very rich mutton broth, but either of the former are preferable; then put on a half cup of rice in a pint of rich milk, and grate into it the white part and root of two heads of celery. Let the rice milk cook very slowly at the back of the stove, adding more milk before it gets at all stiff; when tender enough to mash through a coarse sieve or fine colander add it to the stock, which must have been strained and be quite free from sediment, season with salt and a little *white* pepper or cayenne, boil all together gently a few minutes. It should look like rich cream, and be strongly flavored with celery. Of course the quantity of rice, milk, and celery must depend on the quantity of stock you have. I have given the proportion for one quart, which, with the milk, etc., added, would make about three pints of soup.

CHAPTER X.

SAUCES.

TALLEYRAND said England was a country with twenty-four religions and only one sauce. He might have said two sauces, and he would have been literally right as regards both England and America. Everything is served with brown sauce or white sauce. And how often the white sauce is like bookbinder's paste, the brown, a bitter, tasteless brown mess! Strictly speaking, perhaps, the French have but two sauces either, *espagnole*, or brown sauce, and white sauce, which they call the mother sauces; but what changes they ring on these mother sauces! The espagnole once made, with no two meats is it served alike in flavor, and in this matter of flavor the artist appears. In making brown sauce for any purpose, bethink yourself of anything there may be in your store-room with which to vary its flavor, taking care that it shall agree with the meat for which it is intended. The ordinary cook flies at once to Worcestershire or Harvey sauce, which are excellent at times, but "*toujours perdrix*" is not always welcome. A pinch of mushroom powder, or a few chopped oysters, are excellent with beef or veal; so will be a spoonful of Montpellier butter stirred in, or curry, not enough to yellow the sauce, but enough to give a dash of piquancy. A pickled walnut chopped, or a gherkin or two, go admirably with mutton or pork chops. In short, this is just where imagination and brains will tell in cooking, and little essays of invention may be tried with profit. But beware of trying too much; make yourself perfect in one thing before venturing on another.

ESPAGNOLE, or brown sauce, is simply a rich stock well flavored with vegetables and herbs, and thickened with a piece of *roux* or with brown flour.

WHITE SAUCE is one of those things we rarely find perfectly made; bad, it is the *ne plus ultra* of badness; good, it is delicious. Those who have tried to have it good, and failed, I beg to try the following method of making it: Take an ounce and a half of butter and a scant tablespoonful of flour, mix both with a spoon into a paste; when smooth add half a pint of warm milk, a *small* teaspoonful of salt, and the sixth part of one of *white* pepper; set it on the fire till it boils, and is thick enough to mask the back of the spoon transparently; then add a squeeze of lemon juice, and another ounce and a half of fresh butter; stir this till quite blended. This sauce is the foundation for many others, and, for some purposes, the beaten yolk of an egg is introduced when just off the boil. Capers may be added to it, or chopped mushrooms, or chopped celery, or oysters, according to the use for which it is intended. The object of adding the second butter is because boiling takes away the flavor of butter; by stirring half of it in, without boiling, you retain it.

CHAPTER XI.

WARMING OVER.

HASH is a peculiarly American institution. In no other country is every remnant of cold meat turned into that one unvarying dish. What do I say? *remnants* of cold meat! rather *joints* of cold meat, a roast of beef of which the tenderloin had sufficed for the first day's dinner, the leg of mutton from which a few slices only have been taken, the fillet of veal, available for so many delicate dishes, all are ruthlessly turned into the all-pervading hash. The curious thing is that people are not fond of it. Men exclaim against it, and its name stinks in the nostrils of those unhappy ones whose home is the boarding-house.

Yet hash in itself is not a bad dish; when I say it is a peculiarly *American* institution, I mean, that when English people speak of hash, they mean something quite different—meat warmed in slices. Our hash, in its best form—that is, made with nice gravy, garnished with sippets of toast and pickles, surrounded with mashed potatoes or rice—is dignified abroad by the name of *mince*, and makes its appearance as an elegant little *entrée*. Nor would it be anathematized in the way it is with us, if it were only occasionally introduced. It is the familiarity that has led to contempt. "But what shall I do?" asks the young wife distressfully;

"John likes joints, and he and I and Bridget can't possibly eat a roast at a meal."

Very true; and it is to just such perplexed young housekeepers that I hope this chapter will be especially useful—that is to say, small families with moderate means and a taste for good things. In this, as in many other ways, large families are easier to cater for; they can consume the better part of a roast at a meal, and the remains it is no great harm to turn into hash, although even they might, with little trouble and expense, have agreeable variety introduced into their bill of fare.

In England and America there is great prejudice against warmed-over food, but on the continent one eats it half the time in some of the most delicious-made dishes without suspecting it. Herein lies the secret. With us and our transatlantic cousins the warming over is so artlessly done, that the *hard* fact too often stares at us from out the watery expanse in which it reposes.

One great reason of the failure to make warmed-over meat satisfactory is the lack of gravy. On the goodness of this (as well as its presence) depends the success of your *réchauffé*.

The glaze, for which I have given the recipe, renders you at all times independent in this respect, but at the same time it should not alone be depended on. Every drop of what remains in the dish from the roast should be saved, and great care be taken of all scraps, bones, and gristle, which should be carefully boiled down to save the necessity of flying to the glaze for every purpose. I will here give several recipes, which I think may be new to many readers.

SALMI OF COLD MEAT is exceedingly good. Melt butter in a saucepan, if for quite a small dish two ounces will be sufficient; when melted, stir in a little flour to thicken; let it brown, but not burn, or, if you are preparing the dish in haste, put in some brown flour; then add a glass of white or red wine and a cup of broth, or a cup of water and a slice of glaze, a sprig or two of thyme, parsley, a small onion, chopped, and one bay leaf, pepper, and salt. Simmer all thoroughly (all savory dishes to which wine is added should simmer long enough for the distinct "winey" flavor to disappear, only the strength and richness remaining). Strain this when simmered half an hour and lay in the cold meat. Squeeze in a little lemon juice and draw the stew-pan to the back of the stove, but where it will cook no longer, or the meat will harden. Serve on toast, and pour the sauce over. A glass of brandy added to this dish when the meat goes in is a great addition, if an extra fine salmi is desired. By not allowing the flour and butter to brown and using white wine, this is a very fine sauce in which to warm cold chicken, veal, or any *white* meat.

BŒUF À LA JARDINIÈRE.—Put in a fireproof dish if you have it, or a thick saucepan, a pint of beef broth, a small bunch each of parsley, chervil, tarragon—very little of this—shallot or onion, capers, pickled gherkins, of each or any a teaspoonful chopped fine; roll a large tablespoonful of butter with a dessert-spoonful of brown flour, stir it in; then take slices of underdone beef, with a blunt knife hack each slice all over in fine dice, but not to separate or cut up the slices; then pepper and salt each one and lay it in with the herbs, sprinkle a layer of herbs over the beef and cover closely; then stand the dish in the oven to slowly cook for an hour, or, if you use a stew-pan, set in a pan of boiling water on the stove for an hour where the water will just boil. Serve on a dish surrounded with young carrots and turnips if in season, or old ones cut.

BEEF AU GRATIN.—Cut a little fat bacon or pork very thin, sprinkle on it chopped parsley, onion, and mushrooms (mushroom powder will do) and bread-crumbs; then put in layers of beef, cut thick, and well and closely hacked, then another layer of bacon or pork cut thin as a wafer, and of seasoning, crumbs last; pour over enough broth or gravy to moisten well, in which a little brandy or wine may be added if an especially good dish is desired; bake slowly an hour.

PSEUDO BEEFSTEAK.—Cut cold boiled or roast beef in thick slices, broil slowly, lay in a *hot* dish in which you have a large spoonful of Montpellier butter melted, sprinkle a little mushroom powder if you desire, and garnish with fried potato.

CUTLETS À LA JARDINIÈRE.—Trim some thick cutlets from a cold leg of mutton, or chops from the loin, dip them in frying batter, *à la Carême*, fry crisp and quickly, and serve wreathed round green peas, or a ragout made as follows: Take young carrots, turnips, green peas, white beans; stew gently in a little water to which the bones of the meat and trimmings have been added (and which must be carefully removed not to disfigure the vegetables). Encircle this ragout with the fried cutlets, and crown with a cauliflower.

CROMESQUIS OF LAMB is a Polish recipe. Cut some underdone lamb—mutton will of course do—quite small; also some mushrooms, cut small, or the powder. Put in a saucepan a piece of glaze the size of a pigeon's egg, with a *little* water or broth, warm it and thicken with yolks of two eggs, just as you would make boiled custard, that is, without letting it come to the boil, or it will curdle; then add the mushrooms and meat, let all get cold, and divide it into small pieces, roll in bread-crumbs sifted, then in egg, then in crumbs again, and fry in very hot fat; or you may, *after* rolling in bread-crumbs, lay each piece in a spoon and dip it into frying batter; let the extra batter run off, and drop the cromesquis into the hot fat. These will be good made of beef and rolled up in a bard of fat pork cut thin, and fried; serve with sauce piquant made thus: Take some chopped parsley, onion, and pickled cucumbers, simmer till tender, and thicken with an equal quantity of butter and flour. Of course your own brightness will tell you that, if you are in haste, a spoonful of Montpellier butter, the same of flour, melted in a little water, to which you add a teaspoonful of vinegar, will make an excellent sauce piquant, and this same is excellent for anything fried, as breaded chops, croquettes, etc. I may here say, that where two or three herbs are mentioned as necessary, for instance, parsley, tarragon, and chervil, if you have no tarragon you must leave it out, or chervil the same. It is only a matter of flavoring, at the same time *flavor* is a great deal, and these French herbs give that indescribable *cachet* to a dish which is one of the secrets of French cooking. Therefore if you are a wise matron you will have a supply on hand, even if only bought dry from the druggist.

MIROTON OF BEEF.—Peel and cut into thin slices two large onions, put them in a stew-pan with two ounces of butter, place it over a slow fire; stir the onions round till they are rather brown, but not in the least burnt; add a teaspoonful of brown flour, mix smoothly, then moisten with half a pint of broth, or water with a little piece of glaze, three salt-spoonfuls of salt unless your broth was salted, then half the quantity or less, two of sugar, and one of pepper. Put in the cold beef, cut in thin slices as lean as possible, let it remain five minutes at the back of the stove; then serve on a very hot dish garnished with fried potatoes, or sippets of toast. To vary the flavor, sometimes put a spoonful of tarragon or plain vinegar, or a teaspoonful of mushroom powder, or a pinch of curry, unless objected to, or a few sweet herbs. In fact, as you may see, variety is as easy to produce as it is rare to meet with in average cooking, and depends more on intelligence and thoughtfulness than on anything else.

The simplest of all ways of warming a joint that is not far cut, is to wrap it in thickly buttered paper, and put it in the oven again, contriving, if possible, to cover it closely, let it remain long enough to get *hot* through, not to cook. By keeping it closely covered it will get hot through in less time, and the steam will prevent it getting hard and dry; make some gravy hot and serve with the meat. If your gravy is good and plentiful, your meat will be as nice as the first day; without gravy it would be an unsatisfactory dish. If you cannot manage to cover the joint in the oven, you may put it in a pot over the fire *without* water, but with a dessert spoonful of vinegar to create steam; let it get hot through, and serve as before.

For the third day the meat may be warmed up in any of the ways I am going to mention, repeating once more, that you must have gravy of some kind, or else carefully make some, with cracked bones, gristle, etc., stewed *long*, and nicely flavored with any kind of sauce.

RAGOUT.—A very nice ragout may be made from cold meat thus: Slice the meat, put it in a stew-pan in which an onion, or several if you like them, has been sliced; squeeze half a lemon into it, or a dessert-spoonful of vinegar, cover closely without water, and when it begins to cook, set the stew-pan at the back of the stove for three quarters of an hour, shaking it occasionally. The onions should now be brown; take out the meat, dredge in a little flour, stir it round, and add a cup of gravy, pepper, salt, and a small quantity of any sauce or flavoring you prefer; stew gently a minute or two, then put the meat back to get hot, and serve; garnish with sippets of toast, or pickles.

A NICE LITTLE BREAKFAST DISH is made thus: Cut two long slices of cold meat and three of bread, buttered thickly, about the same shape and size; season the meat with pepper, salt, and a little finely chopped parsley; or, if it is veal, a little chopped ham; then lay one slice of bread between two of meat, and have the other two slices outside; fasten together with short wooden skewers. If you have a quick oven, put it in; and take care to baste with butter thoroughly, that the bread may be all over crisp and brown. If you can't depend on your oven, fry it in very hot fat as you would crullers; garnish with sprigs of parsley, and serve very hot.

TO WARM A GOOD-SIZED PIECE OF BEEF.—Trim it as much like a thick fillet as you can; cut it horizontally half way through, then scoop out as much as you can of the meat from the inside of each piece. Chop the meat fine that you have thus scooped out, season with a little finely chopped parsley and thyme, a shred of onion, if you like it; or if you have celery boil a little of the coarser part till tender, chop it and add as much bread finely crumbled as you have meat, and a good piece of butter; add pepper and salt, and make all into a paste with an egg, mixed with an equal quantity of gravy or milk; fill up the hollow in the meat and tie, or still better, sew it together. You may either put this in a pot with a slice of pork or bacon, and a cup of gravy; or you may brush it over with beaten egg, cover it with crumbs, and pour over these a cup of butter, melted, so that it moistens every part; and bake it, taking care to baste well while baking; serve with nice gravy.

BEEF OLIVES are no novelty to the ear, but it is a novel thing to find them satisfactory to the palate.

Take some stale bread-crumbs, an equal quantity of beef finely chopped, some parsley, and thyme; a little scraped ham if you have it, a few chives, or a slice of onion, all chopped small as possible; put some butter in a pan, and let this force-meat just simmer, *not fry*, in it for ten minutes. While this is cooking, cut some underdone oblong slices of beef about half an inch thick, hack it with a sharp knife on *both sides;* then mix the cooked force-meat with the yolk of an egg and a tablespoonful of gravy; put a spoonful of this paste in the center of each slice of meat and tie it up carefully in the shape of an egg. Then if you have some nice gravy, thicken it with a piece of butter rolled in flour, roll each olive slightly in flour and lay it in the gravy and let it very gently *simmer* for half an hour. A few chopped oysters added to the gravy will be a great addition. Or you may lay each olive on a thin slice of fat pork, roll it up, tie it, dip it in flour, and bake in a quick oven until beautifully brown.

TO WARM OVER COLD MUTTON.—An excellent and simple way is to cut it, if loin, into chops, or leg, into thick collops, and dip each into egg well beaten with a tablespoonful of milk, then in *fine* bread-crumbs and fry in plenty of *very hot* fat.

If your crumbs are not very fine and even, the larger crumbs will fall off, and the appearance be spoilt. These chops will be almost as nice, if quickly fried, as fresh cooked ones. They will also be excellent if, instead of being breaded, they are dipped into thick batter (see recipe) and fried brown in the same way. This method answers for any kind of meat, chicken thus warmed over being especially good. The batter, or egg and bread-crumbs form a sort of crust which keeps it tender and juicy. Any attempt to fry cold meat without either results in a hard, stringy, uneatable dish.

WHITE MEAT OF ANY KIND is excellent warmed over in a little milk, in which you have cut a large onion, and, if you like it, a slice of salt pork or ham, and a little sliced cucumber, if it is summer; thicken with the yolks of one or two eggs, added after the whole has simmered twenty minutes; take care the egg thickens in the gravy, but does not *boil*, or it will curdle. If it is in winter, chop a teaspoonful of pickled cucumber or capers and add just on going to table. In summer when you have the sliced cucumber, squeeze half a lemon into the gravy, the last thing, to give the requisite dash of acid. You may vary the above by adding sometimes a few chopped oysters; at others, mushrooms, or celery. The last must be put in with the onion and before the meat.

DEVILED MEAT.—Our better halves are usually fond of this, especially for breakfast or lunch.

For this dish take a pair of turkey or chicken drumsticks or some nice thick wedges of underdone beef or mutton, score them deeply with a knife and rub them over with a sauce made thus: A teaspoonful of vinegar, the same of Harvey or Worcestershire sauce, the same of mustard, a *little* cayenne, and a tablespoonful of salad oil, or butter melted; mix all till like cream, and take care your meat is thoroughly moistened all over with the mixture, then rub your gridiron with butter. See that the fire is clear, and while the gridiron is getting hot, chop a teaspoonful of parsley very fine, mix it up with a piece of butter the size of a walnut, and lay this in a dish which you will put to get hot. Then put the meat to be grilled on the fire and turn often, so that it will not burn; when hot through and brown, lay it in the hot dish, lay another hot dish over it, and serve as quickly as possible with hot plates.

Or the grill may be served with what Soyer calls his *Mephistophelian sauce,* which he especially designed for serving with deviled meats. Chop six shallots or small onions, wash and press them in the corner of a clean cloth, put them in a stew-pan with half a wineglass of chili vinegar (pepper sauce), a chopped clove, a tiny bit of garlic, two bay leaves, an ounce of glaze; boil all together ten minutes; then add four tablespoonfuls of tomato sauce, a *little* sugar, and ten of broth thickened with roux (or water will do if you have no broth).

It will be remarked that in many French recipes a *little* sugar is ordered. This is not meant to sweeten, or even be perceptible; but it enriches, softens, tones, as it were, the other ingredients as salt does.

SOYER'S FRITADELLA (twenty recipes in one).—Put half a pound of bread-crumb to soak in a pint of cold water; take the same quantity of any kind of roast, or boiled meat, with a little fat, chop it fine, press the bread in a clean cloth to extract the water; put in a stew-pan two ounces of butter, a tablespoonful of chopped onions; fry two minutes and stir, then add the bread, stir and fry till rather dry, then the meat; season with a teaspoonful of salt, half of pepper, and a little grated nutmeg, and lemon peel; stir continually till very hot, then add two eggs, one at a time; mix well and pour on a dish to get cold. Then take a piece, shape it like a small egg, flatten it a little, egg and bread-crumb it all over, taking care to keep in good shape. Do all the same way, then put into a frying-pan a quarter of a pound of lard or dripping, let it get hot, and put in the pieces, and sauté (or as we call it "*fry*") them a fine yellow brown. Serve very hot with a border of mashed potatoes, or any garniture you fancy. Sauce piquant, or not, as you please.

The above can be made with any kind of meat, poultry, game, fish, or even vegetables; hard eggs, or potatoes, may be introduced in small quantities, and they may be fried instead of sautéed (frying in the French and strict sense, meaning as I need hardly say, entire immersion in very hot fat). To *fry* them you require at least two pounds of fat in your pan.

Oysters or lobsters prepared as above are excellent.

Boileau says, "*Un diner réchauffé ne valut jamais rien.*" But I think a good French cook of the present day would make him alter his opinion.

Indeed Savarin quotes a friend of his own, a notable gourmand, who considered spinach cooked on Monday only reached perfection the following Saturday, having each day of the week been warmed up with butter, and each day gaining succulence and a more marrowy consistency.

The only trouble I find in relation to this part of my present task is the difficulty of knowing when to leave off. There are so many ways of warming meats to advantage—and in every one way there is the suggestion for another—that I suffer from an *embarras de richesse*, and have had difficulty in selecting. Dozens come to my mind, blanquettes, patties, curries, as I write; but as this is not, I have said, to be a recipe book, I forbear. Of one thing I am quite sure : when women once know how to make nice dishes of cold meat they will live well where they now live badly, and for less money; and "hash" will be relegated to its proper place as an occasional and acceptable dish.

CHAPTER XII.

ON FRIANDISES.

"Le rôle du gourmand finit avec l'entremets, et celui du friand commence au dessert.—*Grimod de la Reyniere.*

AMERICAN ladies, as a rule, excel in cake making and preserving, and I feel that on that head I have very little to teach; indeed, were they as accomplished in all branches of cooking as in making dainty sweet dishes this book would be uncalled for.

Yet, notwithstanding their undoubted taste and ability in making "*friandises,*" it seems to me a few recipes borrowed from what the French call *la grande cuisine,* and possible of execution at home, will be welcome to those who wish to vary the eternal ice cream and charlotte russe, with other sweets more elegant and likely to be equally popular.

ICED SOUFFLÉ À LA BYRON.—One pint of sugar syrup of 32 degrees (get this at a druggist's if you do not understand sugar boiling), three gills of strained raspberry juice, one lemon, one gill of maraschino, fifteen yolks of eggs, two ounces of chocolate drops, half a pint of very thick cream whipped.

Method of making this and the next recipe is as follows: Mix the syrup and yolks of eggs, strain into a warm bowl, add the raspberry and lemon juice and maraschino, whisk till it creams well, then take the bowl out of the hot water and whisk ten minutes longer; add the chocolate drops and whipped cream; lightly fill a case or mold, and set in a freezer for two hours, then cover the surface with lady-fingers (or sponge cake) dried in the oven a pale brown, and rolled. Serve at once.

Another frozen *soufflé* is as follows:

One pint of syrup, 32 degrees, half a pint of noyeau, half a pint of cherry juice, two ounces of bruised macaroons, half a pint of thick cream whipped, made in the same way as the last. I may here say that the fruit juices can be procured now at all good druggists, so that these *soufflés* are very attainable in winter, and as noyeau and maraschino do not form part of the stores in a family of small means, I will give in this chapter recipes for the making of very fair imitations of the genuine *liqueurs*.

BISCUIT GLACÉ À LA CHARLES DICKENS.—One pint of syrup (32°), fifteen yolks of eggs, three gills of peach pulp, colored pink with cochineal, one gill of noyeau, half a pint of thick cream, and a little chocolate water-ice, made with half a pint of syrup and four ounces of the best chocolate smoothly mixed and frozen ready.

Mix syrup, yolks, peach pulps, noyeau, and a few drops of vanilla, whip high; mix with the whipped cream, and set in ice for one hour and a half in brick-shaped molds, then turn out (if very firm), and cut in slices an inch thick, and coat them all over, or on top and sides, with the chocolate ice, smoothing with a knife dipped in cold water; serve in paper cases.

BISCUIT GLACÉ À LA THACKERAY.—One pint of syrup (32°), one pint of strawberry pulp, fifteen yolks of eggs, one ounce of vanilla sugar (flavor a little sugar with vanilla), half a pint of thick cream.

Mix syrup, yolks, strawberry, and vanilla sugar, whipping as before, then add the whipped cream lightly; fill paper cases, either round or square; surround each with a band of stiff paper, to reach half an inch above the edge of the case, the bands to be pinned together to secure them; place them in a freezer. When about to send to table, remove the bands of paper, and cover with macaroons bruised fine and browned in the oven. The bands of paper are meant to give the biscuit the appearance of having risen while supposed to bake.

These delicious ices were invented by Francatelli, the Queen of England's chief cook, to do homage to the different great men whose names they bear, on the occasion of preparing dinners given in their honor. They read as if somewhat intricate, but any lady who has ever had ice cream made at home, and had the patience to make charlotte russe, need not shrink appalled before these novelties, or fear for a successful result.

Baba is a cake many call for at a confectioner's, yet few, if any one, attempts to make it at home. That the recipes generally offered do not lead to success may be one reason, and I offer the following, quite sure, if accurately followed, such a baba will result as never was eaten outside of Paris.

BABA.—One pound of flour; take one quarter of it, and make a sponge with half an ounce of compressed yeast and a little warm water, set it to rise, make a hole in the rest of the flour, add to it ten ounces of butter, three eggs, and a dessert-spoonful of sugar, a little salt, unless your butter salts it enough, which is generally the case. Beat all together well, then add five more eggs, one at a time, that is to say, add one egg and beat well, then another and beat again, and so on until the five are used. When the paste leaves the bowl it is beaten enough, but not before; then add the sponge to it, and a large half ounce of citron chopped, the same of currants, and an ounce and a half of sultana raisins, seedless. Let it rise to twice its size, then bake it in an oven of dark yellow paper heat; the small round babas are an innovation of the pastry-cook to enable him to sell them uncut. But the baba proper should be baked in a large, deep, upright tin, such as a large charlotte russe mold, when they keep for several days fresh, and if they get stale, make delicious fritters, soaked in sherry and dipped in frying batter.

In some cases, however, it may be preferred to make them as usually seen at French pastry cooks; for this purpose you require a dozen small-sized *round* charlotte russe molds, which fill half full only, as they rise very much; bake these in a hotter oven, light brown paper heat; try with a twig as you would any other cake, if it comes out dry it is done; then prepare a syrup as follows: Boil half pound of sugar in a pint of water, add to this the third of a pint of rum, and some apricot pulp—peach will of course do—and boil all together a few minutes; pour this half an inch deep in a dish, and stand the cake or cakes in it; it should drink up all the syrup, you may also sprinkle some over it. If any syrup remains, use it to warm over your cake when stale, instead of the sherry.

Baba was introduced into France by Stanislas Leczinski, king of Poland, and the father-in-law of Louis XIV.; and his Polish royal descendants still use with it, says Carême, a syrup made of Malaga wine and one sixth part of *eau de tanaisie*.

But, although our forefathers seemed to have relished

tansy very much, to judge from old recipe books, I doubt if such flavoring would be appreciated in our time.

SAVARINS—commonly called wine cake by New York pastry cooks—are made as follows :

One pound of flour, of which take one quarter to make a sponge, using half an ounce of German compressed yeast, and a little warm milk ; when it has risen to twice its bulk, add one gill of hot milk, two eggs, and the rest of the flour ; mix well ; then add one more egg and beat, another, still beating; then add three quarters of a pound of fresh butter, a quarter of an ounce of salt, half an ounce of sugar, and half a gill of hot milk, beat well; then add eggs, one at a time, beating continually, until you have used five more. Cut in small dice three ounces of candied orange peel; butter a tin, which should be deep and straight-sided—a tin pudding boiler is not a bad thing—and sprinkle with chopped almonds. Fill the mold half full, and when risen to twice its bulk, bake in a moderate oven, dark yellow paper heat. When served, this cake should stand in a dish of syrup, flavored with rum, as for baba, or with sherry wine.

BOUCHÉES DES DAMES, a very ornamental and delicious little French cake, is sufficiently novel to deserve a place here, I think. Make any nice drop cake batter (either sponge, or sponge with a little butter in it I prefer) ; drop one on buttered paper and bake ; if it runs, beat in a *little* more flour and sugar, but not much, or your cakes will be brittle ; they should be the size, when done, of a fifty-cent piece; and I find half a teaspoonful of batter dropped generally makes them about right. Have a tin cutter or tin box lid, if you have no cutter so small, about the size, and with it trim each cake when baked ;

then take half the number and spread some with a very thin layer of red currant jelly, others with peach or raspberry; then on each so spread put a cake that is unspread, thus making a tiny sandwich or jelly cake. If you have different sorts of jelly, put each separate, as you must adapt the flavor of your icing to the jelly. For red currant, ice with chocolate icing. Recipes for icing are so general that I refer you to your cookery book. Those with peach may have white icing, flavored with almond, or with rum, beating in a little more sugar if the flavoring dilutes your icing too much. Almond flavoring goes well with raspberry. Cakes with raspberry jelly or jam should be iced pink, coloring the icing with prepared cochineal or cranberry juice. Thus you have your cakes brown, pink, and white, which look very pretty mixed.

The process of icing is difficult to do after they are put together, but they are much handsomer this way, and keep longer. You require, to accomplish it, a good quantity of each kind of icing, and a number of little wooden skewers; stick one into each cake and dip it in the icing, let it run off, then stand the other end of the skewer in a box of sand or granulated sugar. The easiest way is to ice each half cake before putting in the jelly; when the icing is hard spread with jelly, and put together.

CURAÇOA may be successfully imitated by pouring over eight ounces of the *thinly* pared rind of very ripe oranges a pint of boiling water, cover, and let it cool; then add two quarts of brandy, or strong French spirit, cover closely, and let it stand fourteen days, shaking it every day. Make a clarified syrup of two pounds of sugar into one pint of water, well boiled; strain the brandy into it, leaving it covered close another day. Rub up in a mortar one drachm of potash, with a teaspoonful of the liqueurs; when well blended, put this into the liqueur, and in the same way pound and add a drachm of alum, shake well, and in an hour or two filter through thin muslin. Ready for use in a week or two.

MARASCHINO.—Bruise slightly a dozen cherry kernels, put them in a deep jar with the outer rind of three oranges and two lemons, cover with two quarts of gin, then add syrup and leave it a fortnight, as for curaçoa. Stir syrup and spirit together, leave it another day, run it through a jelly bag, and bottle. Ready to use in ten days.

NOYEAU.—Blanch and pound two pounds of bitter almonds, or four of peach kernels; put to them a gallon of spirit or brandy, two pounds of white sugar candy—or sugar will do—a grated nutmeg, and a pod of vanilla; leave it three weeks covered close, then filter and bottle; but do not use it for three months. To be used with caution.

CHAPTER XIII.

FRENCH CANDY AT HOME.

THIS chapter I shall have to make one of recipes chiefly, for it treats of a branch of cooking not usually found in cookery books, or at least there is seldom anything on the art of confectionery beyond molasses or cream taffy and nougat. These, therefore, I shall not touch upon, but rather show you how to make the expensive French candies.

The great art of making these exquisite candies is in boiling the sugar, and it is an art easily acquired with patience.

Put into a marbleized saucepan (by long experience in sugar-boiling I find them less likely to burn even than brass, and I keep one for the purpose) one pound of sugar and half a pint of water; when it has boiled ten minutes begin to try it; have a bowl of water with a piece of ice near you, and drop it from the end of a spoon. When it falls to the bottom, and you can take it up and make it into a softish ball (not at all sticky) between your thumb and finger, it is at the right point; remove it from the fire to a cold place; when cool, if perfectly right, a thin jelly-like film will be over the surface, *not a sugary one;* if it is sugary, and you want your candy very creamy, you must add a few spoonfuls of water, return to the fire and boil again, going through the same process of trying it. You must be careful that there is not the least inclination to be brittle in the ball of candy you take from the water; if so, it is boiled a degree too high; put a little water to bring it back again, and try once more. A speck of cream of tartar is useful in checking a tendency in the syrup to go to sugar. When you have your sugar boiled just right set it to cool, and when you can bear your finger in it, begin to beat it with a spoon-; in ten minutes it will be a white paste resembling lard, which you will find you can work like bread dough. This, then, is your foundation, called by French confectioners *fondant;* with your *fondant* you can work marvels. But to begin with the simplest French candies.

Take a piece of *fondant,* flavor part of it with vanilla, part of it with lemon, color yellow (see coloring candies), and another part with raspberry, color pink; make these into balls, grooved cones, or anything that strikes your fancy, let them stand till they harden, they are then ready for use.

Take another part of your *fondant,* have some English walnuts chopped, flavor with vanilla and color pink; work the walnuts into the paste as you would fruit into a loaf cake; when mixed, make a paper case an inch wide and deep, and three or four inches long; oil it; press the paste into it, and when firm turn it out and cut into cubes. Or, instead of walnuts, use chopped almonds, flavor with vanilla, and leave the *fondant* white. This makes VANILLA ALMOND CREAM.

TUTTI FRUTTI CANDY.—Chop some almonds, citron, a *few* currants, and seedless raisins; work into some *fondant,* flavor with rum and lemon, thus making Roman punch, or with vanilla or raspberry; press into the paper forms as you did the walnut cream. You see how you can ring the changes on these bars, varying the flavoring, inventing new combinations, etc.

FONDANT PANACHÉ.—Take your *fondant,* divide it in three equal parts, color one pink and flavor as you choose, leave the other white and flavor also as you please; but it must agree with the pink, and both must agree with the next, which is chocolate. Melt a little unsweetened chocolate by setting it in a saucer over the boiling kettle, then take enough of it to make your third piece of *fondant* a fine brown; now divide the white into two parts; make each an inch and a half wide, and as long as it will; do the same with the chocolate *fondant;* then take the pink, make it the same width and length, but of course, not being divided, it will be twice as thick; now butter slightly the back of a plate, or, better still, get a few sheets of waxed paper from the confectioner's; lay one strip of the chocolate on it, then a strip of white on that, then the pink, the other white, and lastly the chocolate again; then lightly press them to make them adhere, but not to squeeze them out of shape. You have now an oblong brick of parti-colored candy; leave it for a few hours to harden, then trim it neatly with a knife and cut it crosswise into slices half an inch think, lay on waxed paper to dry, turning once in a while, and pack away in boxes.

If your *fondant* gets very hard while you work, stand it over hot water a few minutes.

Creamed candies are very fashionable just now, and, your *fondant* once ready, are very easy to make.

CREAM WALNUTS.—Make ready some almonds, some walnuts in halves, some hazelnuts, or anything of the sort you fancy; let them be very dry. Take *fondant* made from a pound of sugar, set it in a bowl in a saucepan of boiling water, stirring it till it is like cream. Then having flavored it with vanilla or lemon, drop in your nuts one by one, taking them out with the other hand on the end of a fork, resting it on the edge of your bowl to drain for a second, then drop the nut on to a waxed or buttered paper neatly. If the nut shows through the cream it is too hot; take it out of the boiling water and beat till it is just thick enough to mask the nut entirely, then return it to the boiling water, as it cools very rapidly and becomes unmanageable, when it has to be warmed over again.

VERY FINE CHOCOLATE CREAMS are made as follows: Boil half a pound of sugar with three tablespoonfuls of thick cream till it makes a *soft* ball in water, then let it cool. When cool beat it till it is very white, flavor with a few drops of vanilla and make it into balls the size of a large pea; then take some unsweetened chocolate warmed, mix it with a piece of *fondant* melted—there should be more chocolate than sugar—and when quite smooth and thick enough to mask the cream, drop them in from the end of a fork, take them out, and drop on to wax paper.

Another very fine candy to be made without heat, and therefore convenient for hot weather, is made as follows:

PUNCH DROPS.—Sift some powdered sugar. Have ready some fine white gum-arabic, put a tablespoonful with the sugar (say half a pound of sugar), and make it into a firm paste; if too wet, add more sugar, flavor with lemon and a tiny speck of tartaric acid or a very little lemon juice. Make the paste into small balls, then take more sugar and make it into icing with a spoonful of Santa Cruz rum and half the white of an egg. Try if it hardens, if not, beat in more sugar and color it a bright pink, then dip each ball in the pink icing and harden on wax paper. These are very novel, beautiful to look at, and the flavors may vary to taste.

TO MAKE COCHINEAL COLORING WHICH IS QUITE HARMLESS.—Take one ounce of powdered cochineal, one ounce of cream of tartar, two drachms of alum, half a pint of water; boil the cochineal, water, and cream of tartar till reduced to one half, then add the alum, and put up in small bottles for use. Yellow is obtained by the infusion of Spanish saffron in a little water, or a still better one from the grated rind of a ripe orange put into muslin, and a little of the juice squeezed through it.

Be careful in boiling the sugar for *fondant*, not to stir it after it is dissolved; stirring causes it to become rough instead of creamy.

CHAPTER XIV.

A CHAPTER FOR PEOPLE OF VERY SMALL MEANS.

I AM sorry to say in these days this chapter may appeal to many, who are yet not to be called "poor people," who may have been well-to-do and only suffering from the pressure of the times, and for whose cultivated appetites the coarse, substantial food of the laboring man (even if they could buy it) would not be eatable, who must have what they do have good, or starve. But, as some of the things for which I give recipes will seem over-economical for people who can afford to buy meat at least once a day, I advise those who have even fifty dollars a month income to skip it; reminding them, if they do not, "that necessity knows no law."

A bone of soup meat can be got at a good butcher's for ten or fifteen cents, and is about the best investment, for that sum I know of, as two nourishing and savory meals, at least, for four or five persons can be got from it.

Carefully make a nice soup, with plenty of vegetables, rice, or any other thickening you like. Your bone will weigh from four to six pounds, perhaps; put it on with water according to size, and let it boil down slowly until nice and strong. If you have had any scraps of meat or bones, put them also to your soup.

When you serve it, keep back a cup of soup and a few

of the vegetables, and save the meat, from which you can make a very appetizing hash in the following way: Take the meat from the bone, chop it with some cold potatoes and the vegetables you saved from the soup. Cold stewed onions, boiled carrots or turnips, all help to make the dish savory. Chop an onion very fine, unless you have cold ones, a little parsley and thyme, if liked, and sometimes, for variety's sake, if you have it, a pinch of curry powder, not enough to make it hot or yellow, yet to impart piquancy. If you have a tiny bit of fried bacon or cold ham or cold pork, chop it with the other ingredients, mix all well, moisten with the cold soup, and, when nicely seasoned, put the hash into an iron frying-pan, in which you have a little fat made hot; pack it smoothly in, cover it with a pot-lid, and either set it in a hot oven, or leave it to brown on the stove. If there was more soup than enough to moisten the hash, put it on in a tiny saucepan, with a little brown flour made into a paste with butter, add a drop of tomato catsup, or a little stewed tomato, or anything you have for flavoring, and stir till it boils. Then turn the hash out whole on a dish, it should be brown and crisp, pour the gravy you have made round it, and serve. For a change make a pie of the hash, pouring the gravy in through a hole in the top when done.

It is not generally known that a very nice plain paste can be made with a piece of bread dough, to which you have added an egg, and some lard, dripping, or butter. The dripping is particularly nice for the hash pie, and, as you need only a piece of dough as large as an orange, you will probably have enough from the soup, if you skimmed off all the fat before putting the vegetables in (see *pot-au-feu*); work your dripping into the dough, and let it rise well, then roll as ordinary pie-crust. Potato crust is also very good for plain pies of any sort, but as there are plenty of recipes for it, I will not give one here.

One of the very best hashes I ever ate was prepared by a lady who, in better times, kept a very fine table. And she told me there were a good many cold beans in it, well mashed; and often since, when taking "travelers' hash" in an hotel, I have thought of that savory dish with regret.

Instead of making your chopped meat into hash, vary it, by rolling the same mixture into egg-shaped pieces, or flat cakes, flouring them, and frying them nicely in very hot fat; pieces of pork or bacon fried and laid round will help out the dish, and be an improvement to what is already very good.

To return once more to the soup bone. If any one of your family is fond of marrow, seal up each end of the bone with a paste made of flour and water. When done, take off the paste, and remove the marrow. Made very hot, and spread on toast, with pepper and salt, it will be a relish for some one's tea or breakfast.

In this country there is a prejudice against sheep's liver; while in England, where beef liver is looked upon as too coarse to eat (and falls to the lot of the "catsmeat man," or cat butcher), sheep's is esteemed next to calf's, and it is, in fact, more delicate than beef liver. The nicest way to cook it is in very *thin* slices (not the inch-thick pieces one often sees), each slice dipped in flour and fried in pork or bacon fat, and pork or bacon served with it. But the more economical way is to put it in a pan, dredge it with flour, pin some fat pork over it, and set it in a hot oven; when very brown take it out;

make nice brown gravy by pouring water in the pan and letting it boil on the stove, stirring it well to dissolve the glaze; pour into the dish, and serve. The heart should be stuffed with bread-crumbs, parsley, thyme, and a *little* onion, and baked separately. Or, for a change, you may chop the liver up with a few sweet herbs and a little pork (onion, or not, as you like), and some bread-crumbs. Put all together in a crock, dredge with flour, cover, and set in a slow oven for an hour and a half; then serve, with toasted bread around the dish.

It is very poor economy to buy inferior meat. One pound of fine beef has more nourishment than two of poor quality. But there is a great difference in prices of different parts of meat, and it is better management to choose the cheap part of fine beef than to buy the sirloin of a poor ox even at the same price; and, by good cooking many parts not usually chosen, and therefore sold cheaply, can be made very good. Yet you must remember, that a piece of meat at seven cents a pound, in which there is at least half fat and bone, such as brisket, etc., is less economical than solid meat at ten or twelve.

Pot roasts are very good for parts of meat not tender enough for roasting, the "cross-rib," as some butchers term it, being very good for this purpose; it is all solid meat, and being very lean, requires a little fat pork, which may be laid at the bottom of the pot; or better still, holes made in the meat and pieces of the fat drawn through, larding in a rough way, so that they cut together. A pot roast is best put on in an iron pot, without water, allowed to get finely brown on one side, then turned, and when thoroughly brown on the other a little water may be added for gravy; chop parsley or any seasoning that is preferred. Give your roast at least three hours to cook. Ox cheek, as the head is called, is very good, and should be very cheap; prepare it thus:

Clean the cheek, soak it in water six hours, and cut the meat from the bones, which break up for soup; then take the meat, cut into neat pieces, put it in an earthen crock, a layer of beef, some thin pieces of pork or bacon, some onions, carrots, and turnips, cut *thin,* or chopped fine, and sprinkled over the meat; also, some chopped parsley, a little thyme, and bay leaf, pepper and salt, and a clove to each layer; then more beef and a little pork, vegetables, and seasoning, as before. When all your meat is in pour over it, if you have it, a tumbler of hard cider and one of water, or else two of water, in which put a half gill of vinegar. If you have no tight-fitting cover to your crock, put a paste of flour and water over it to keep the steam in. Place the crock in a slow oven five or six hours, and when it is taken out remove the crust and skim. Any piece of beef cooked in this way is excellent.

Ox heart is one of the cheapest of dishes, and really remarkably nice, and it is much used by economical people abroad.

The heart should be soaked in vinegar and water three or four hours, then cut off the lobes and gristle, and stuff it with fat pork chopped, bread-crumbs, parsley, thyme, pepper, and salt; then tie it in a cloth and very slowly simmer it (large end up) for two hours; take it up, remove the cloth, and flour it, and roast it a nice brown. Lay in the pan in which it is to be roasted some fat pork to baste it. Any of this left over is excellent hashed, or, warmed in slices with a rich brown gravy, cannot be told from game. Another way is to stuff it with sage and onions. It must always be served *very hot* with hot plates and on a very hot dish.

Fore quarter of mutton is another very economical part of meat, if you get your butcher to cut it so that it may not only be economical, but really afford a choice joint. Do not then let him hack the shoulder across, but, before he does a thing to it, get him to take the shoulder out in a round plate-shaped joint, with knuckle attached; if he does this well, that is, cuts it close to the bone of the ribs, you will have a nice joint; then do not have it chopped at all; this should be roasted in the oven very nicely, and served with onion sauce or stewed onions. If onions are not liked, mashed turnips are the appropriate vegetable. This joint, to be enjoyed, must be properly carved, and that is, across the middle from the edge to the bone, the same as a leg of mutton; and like the leg, you must learn, as I cannot describe it in words, where the bone lies, then have that side nearest you and cut from the opposite side.

You have, besides this joint, another roast from the ribs, or else cut it up into chops till you come to the part under the shoulder; from this the breast should be separated and both either made into a good Irish stew, or the breast prepared alone in a way I shall describe, the neck and thin ribs being stewed or boiled.

The neck of mutton is very tender boiled and served with parsley or caper sauce; the liquor it is boiled in served as broth, with vegetables and rice, or prepared as directed in a former chapter for the broth from leg of mutton.

The mode I am about to give of preparing breast of mutton was told me by a Welsh lady of rank, at whose table I ate it (it appeared as a side dish), and who said, half laughingly, "Will you take some 'fluff'? We are very fond of it, but breast of mutton is such a despised dish I never expect any one else to like it." I took it, on my principle of trying everything, and did find it very good. This lady told me that, having of course a good deal of mutton killed on her father's estate, and the breast being always despised by the servants, she had invented a way of using it to avoid waste. Her way was this:

Set the breast of mutton on the fire whole, just covered with water in which is a little salt. When it comes to the boil draw it back and let it *simmer* three hours; then take it up and draw out the bones, and lay a forcemeat of bread-crumbs, parsley, thyme, chopped suet, salt and pepper all over it; double or roll it, skewer it, and coat it thickly with egg and bread-crumbs; then bake in a moderate oven, basting it often with nice dripping or butter; when nicely brown it is done, and eats like the tenderest lamb. It was, when I saw it, served on a bed of spinach. I like it better on a bed of stewed onions.

I now give some dishes made without meat.

RAGOUT OF CUCUMBER AND ONIONS.—Fry equal quantities of large cucumbers and onions in slices until they are a nice brown. The cucumber will brown more easily if cut up and put to drain some time before using; then flour each slice. When both are brown, pour on them a cup of water, and let them stew for half an hour; then take a good piece of butter in which you have worked a dessert-spoonful of flour (browned); add pepper, salt, and a little tomato catsup or stewed tomato. This is a rich-eating dish if nicely made, and will help out cold meat or a scant quantity of it very well. A little cold meat may be added if you have it.

ONION SOUP.—Fry six large onions cut into slices with a quarter of a pound of butter till they are of a bright brown, then well mix in a tablespoonful of flour, and pour on them rather more than a quart of water. Stew gently until the onions are quite tender, season with a spoonful of salt and a little sugar; stir in quickly a *liaison* made with the yolks of two eggs mixed with a gill of milk or cream (do not let it boil afterwards), put some toast in a tureen, and serve very hot.

PEA SOUP.—Steep some yellow split peas all night, next morning set them on to boil with two quarts of water to a pint of peas; in the water put a tiny bit of soda. In another pot put a large carrot, a turnip, an onion, and a large head of celery, all cut small and covered with water. When both peas and vegetables are tender, put them together, season with salt, pepper, and a little sugar, and let them gently stew till thick enough; then strain through a colander, rubbing the vegetables well, and return to the pot while you fry some sippets of bread a crisp brown; then stir into the soup two ounces of butter in which you have rolled a little flour.

This soup is simply delicious, and the fact of it being *maigre* will not be remembered.

POTATO SOUP is another of this good kind, for meat is scarcely required, so good is it without.

Boil some potatoes, then rub them through a colander into two quarts of hot milk (skimmed does quite well); have some fine-chopped parsley and onion, add both with salt and pepper, stew three quarters of an hour; then stir in a large piece of butter, and beat two eggs with a little cold milk, stir in quickly, and serve with fried bread. There should be potatoes enough to make the soup as thick as cream.

Do not be prejudiced against a dish because there is no meat in it, and you think it cannot be nourishing. This chapter is not written for those with whom meat, or money, is plentiful; and if it be true that man is nourished "not by what he eats, but by what he assimilates," and, according to an American medical authority, "what is eaten with distaste is not assimilated" (Dr. Hall), it follows that an enjoyable dinner, even without meat, will be more nourishing than one forced down because it lacks savor; that potato soup will be more nourishing than potatoes and butter, with a cup of milk to drink, because more enjoyable. Yet it costs no more, for the soup can be made without the eggs if they are scarce.

Or say bread and butter and onions. They will not be very appetizing, especially if they had to be a frequent meal, yet onion soup is made from the same materials, and in France is a very favorite dish, even with those well able to put meat in it if they wished.

CHAPTER XV.

A FEW THINGS IT IS WELL TO REMEMBER.

Every housekeeper has pet "wrinkles" of her own which she thinks are especially valuable; some are known to all the world, others are new to many. So it may be with mine; but, on the chance that some few things are as new to my friends as they were to me, I jot them down without any pretense of order or regularity.

Lemons will keep fresher and better in water than any other way. Put them in a crock, cover them with water. They will in winter keep two or three months, and the peel be as fresh as the day they were put in. Take care, of course, that they do not get frosted. In summer change the water twice a week; they will keep a long time.

In grating nutmegs begin at the flower end; if you commence at the other, there will be a hole all the way through.

Tea or coffee made hot (not at all scorched), before water is added, are more fragrant and stronger. Thus, by putting three spoonfuls of tea in the pot and setting in a warm place before infusing, it will be as strong as if you make tea with four spoonfuls without warming it, and much more fragrant.

Vegetables that are strong can be made much milder

by tying a bit of bread in a clean rag and boiling it with them.

Bread dough is just as good made the day before it is used; thus, a small family can have fresh bread one day, rolls the next, by putting the dough in a cold place enveloped in a damp cloth. In winter, kept cold, yet not in danger of freezing, it will keep a week.

Celery seed takes the place of celery for soup or stews when it is scarce; parsley seed of parsley.

Green beans, gherkins, etc., put down when plentiful in layers of rock salt, will keep crisp and green for months, and can be taken out and pickled when convenient.

Lemon or orange peel grated and mixed with powdered sugar and a squeeze of its own juice (the sugar making it into paste) is excellent to keep for flavoring; put it into a little pot and it will keep for a year.

Bread that is very stale may be made quite fresh for an hour or two by dipping it quickly into milk or water, and putting it in a brisk oven till *quite hot through*. It must be eaten at once, or it will be as stale as ever when cold.

Meat to be kept in warm weather should be rubbed over with salad oil, every crevice filled with ginger; meat that is for roasting or frying is much better preserved in this way than with salt; take care that every part of the surface has a coat of oil. Steaks or chops cut off, which always keep badly, should be dipped into warm butter or even dripping, if oil is not handy (the object being to exclude the air), and then hung up till wanted.

Mutton in cold weather should be hung four or five weeks in a place not subject to changes of temperature, and before it is so hung, every crevice filled with ginger and thoroughly dredged with flour, which must be then rubbed in with the hand till the surface is quite dry. This is the English fashion of keeping venison.

It may be useful for those who burn kerosene to know that when their lamps smell, give a bad light, and smoke, it is not necessary to buy new burners. Put the old ones in an old saucepan with water and a tablespoonful of soda, let them boil half an hour, wipe them, and your trouble will be over.

Meat that has become slightly tainted may be quite restored by washing it in water in which is a teaspoonful of borax, cutting away every part in the least discolored.

In summer when meat comes from the butcher's, if it is not going to be used the same day, it should be washed over with vinegar.

Poultry in summer should always have a piece of charcoal tied in a rag placed in the stomach, to be removed before cooking. Pieces of charcoal should also be put in the refrigerator and changed often.

Oyster shells put one at a time in a stove that is "clinkered" will clean the bricks entirely. They should be put in when the fire is burning brightly.

Salt and soapstone powder (to be bought at the druggist's) mend fire brick; use equal quantities, make into a paste with water, and cement the brick; they will be as strong as new ones.

Ink spilled on carpets may be entirely removed by rubbing while wet with blotting paper, using fresh as it soils.

CHAPTER XVI.

ON SOME TABLE PREJUDICES.

MANY people have strong prejudices against certain things which they have never even tasted, or which they do frequently take and like as a part of something else, without knowing it. How common it is to hear and see untraveled people declare that they dislike garlic, and could not touch anything with it in. Yet those very people will take Worcestershire sauce, in which garlic is actually predominant, with everything they eat; and think none but English pickles eatable, which owe much of their excellence to the introduction of a *soupçon* of garlic. Therefore I beg those who actually only know garlic from hearsay abuse of it, or from its presence on the breath of some inveterate garlic eater, to give it a fair trial when it appears in a recipe. It is just one of those things that require the most delicate handling, for which the French term a "*suspicion*" is most appreciated; it should only be a suspicion, its presence should never be pronounced. As Blot once begged his readers, "Give garlic a fair trial in a *rémolade* sauce." (Montpellier butter beaten into mayonnaise is a good *rémolade* for cold meat or fish.)

Curry is one of those things against which many are strongly prejudiced, and I am inclined to think it is quite an acquired taste, but a taste which is an enviable one to its possessors; for them there is endless variety in all they eat. The capabilities of curry are very little known in this country, and, as the taste for it is so limited, I will not do more in its defense than indicate a pleasant use to which it may be put, and in which form it would be a welcome condiment to many to whom "a curry," pure and simple, would be obnoxious. I once knew an Anglo-Indian who used curry as most people use cayenne; it was put in a pepper-box, and with it he would at times pepper his fish or kidneys, even his eggs. Used in this way, it imparts a delightful piquancy to food, and is neither hot nor " spicy."

Few people are so prejudiced as the English generally, and the stay-at-home Americans; but the latter are to be taught by travel, the Englishman rarely.

The average Briton leaves his island shores with the conviction that he will get nothing fit to eat till he gets back, and that he will have to be uncommonly careful once across the channel, or he will be having fricasseed frogs palmed on him for chicken. Poor man! in his horror of frogs, he does not know that the Paris restaurateur who should give the costly frog for chicken, would soon end in the bankruptcy court.

"If I could only get a decent dinner, a good roast and plain potato, I would like Paris much better," said an old Englishman to me once in that gay city.

"But surely you can."

"No; I have been to restaurants of every class, and called for beefsteak and roast beef, but have never got the real article, although it's my belief," said he, leaning forward solemnly, "that I have eaten *horse* three times this week." Of course the Englishman of rank, who has spent half his life on the continent, is not at all the *average* Englishman.

Americans think the hare and rabbits, of which the English make such good use, very mean food indeed, and if they are unprejudiced enough to try them, from the fact that they are never well cooked, they dislike them, which prejudice the English reciprocate by looking on squirrels as being as little fit for food as a rat. And a familiar instance of prejudice from ignorance carried even to insanity, is that of the Irish in 1848, starving rather than eat the "yaller male," sent them by generous American sympathizers; yet they come here and soon get over that dislike. Not so the French, who look on oatmeal and Indian meal as most unwholesome food. "*Ça pése sur l'estomac, ça creuse l'estomac,*" I heard an old Frenchwoman say, trying to dissuade a mother from giving her children mush.

The moral of all of which is, that for our comfort's sake, and the general good we should avoid unreasonable prejudices against unfamiliar food. We of course have a right to our honest dislikes; but to condemn things because we have heard them despised, is prejudice.

CHAPTER XVII.

A CHAPTER OF ODDS AND ENDS—VALEDICTORY.

I HAVE alluded, in an earlier chapter, to the fact that many inexperienced cooks are afraid of altering recipes; a few words on this subject may not be out of place. As a rule, a recipe should be faithfully followed in all important points; for instance, in making soup you cannot, because you are short of the given quantity of meat, put the same amount of water as directed for the full quantity, without damaging your soup; but you may easily reduce water and *every other ingredient* in the same proportion; and, in mere matters of flavoring, you may vary to suit circumstances. If you are told to use cloves, and have none, a bit of mace may be substituted.

If you read a recipe, and it calls for something you have not, consider whether that something has anything to do with the substance of the dish, or whether it is merely an accessory for which something else can be substituted. For instance, if you are ordered to use cream in a sauce, milk with a larger amount of well-washed butter may take its place; but if you are told to use cream for charlotte russe or trifles, there is no way in which you could make milk serve, since it is not an accessory but the chief part of those dishes. For a cake in which cream is used, butter whipped to a cream may take its place. Wine is usually optional in savory dishes; it gives richness only.

Again, in cakes be very careful the exact proportions of flour, eggs, and milk are observed ; of butter you can generally use more or less, having a more or less rich cake in proportion. In any but plain cup cakes (which greatly depend on soda and acid for their lightness) never lessen the allowance of eggs ; never add milk if a cake is too stiff (but an extra egg may always be used), unless milk is ordered in the recipe, when more or less may be used as needed. Flavoring may be always varied.

In reducing a recipe always reduce *every ingredient*, and it can make no difference in the results. Sometimes, in cookery books, you are told to use articles not frequently found in ordinary kitchens; for instance, a larding-needle (although that can be bought for twenty-five cents at any house-furnishing store, and should always be in a kitchen); but, in case you have not one for meat, you may manage by making small cuts and inserting slips of bacon.

Another article that is very useful, but seldom, if ever, to be found in small kitchens, is a salamander ; but when you wish to brown the top of a dish, and putting it in the oven would not do, or the oven is not quick enough to serve, an iron shovel, made nearly red, and a few red cinders in it, is a very good salamander. It must be held over the article that requires browning near enough to color it, yet not to burn.

In the recipes. I have given nothing is required that cannot be obtained, with more or less ease, in New York. For syrups, fruit juices, etc., apply to your druggist; if he has not them he will tell you where to obtain them. We often make up our minds that because a thing is not commonly used in this country, it is impossible to get it. Really there are very few things not to be got in New

York City to the intelligent seeker. You need an article of French or Italian or may be English grocery, that your grocer, a first-class one, perhaps, has not, and you make up your mind you cannot get it. But go into the quarters where French people live, and you can get everything belonging to the French *cuisine*. So prejudiced are the French in favor of the productions of *la belle France*, that they do not believe in our parsley or our chives or garlic or shallots; for I know at least one French grocer who imports them for his customers. On being asked why he brought them from France to a country where those very things were plentiful, he answered:

"Oh, French herbs are much finer."

Needless to say tarragon is one of the herbs so imported, and can thus be bought; but, as several New Jersey truck gardeners grow all kinds of French herbs, they can be got in Washington Market, and most druggists keep them dried; but for salads, Montpellier butter, and some other uses, the dried herb would not do, although for flavoring it would serve; but the far better way is to grow them for yourself, as I have done. Any large seedsman will supply you with burnet, tarragon, and borage (very useful for salads, punch, etc.) seeds, and if you live in the country, have an herb bed; if in town, there are few houses where there is not ground enough to serve for the purpose; but even in these few houses one can have a box of earth in the kitchen window, in which your seeds will flourish.

Parsley is a thing in almost daily request in winter, yet it is very expensive to buy it constantly for the sake of using the small spray that often suffices. It is a good plan, therefore, in fall, to get a few roots, plant them in a pot or box, and they will flourish all winter, if kept where they will not freeze, and be ready for garnishing at any minute.

Always, as far as your means allow, have every convenience for cooking. By having utensils proper for every purpose you save a great deal of work and much vexation of spirit. Yet it should be no excuse for bad work that such utensils are not at hand. A willing and intelligent cook will make the best of what she has. Apropos of this very thing Gouffé relates that a friend of his, an "artist" of renown, was sent for to the chateau of a Baron Argenteuil, who had taken a large company with him, unexpectedly crowding the chateau in every part. He was shown into a dark passage in which a plank was suspended from the ceiling, and told this was to be his kitchen. He had to fashion his own utensils, for there was nothing provided, and his pastry he had to bake in a frying-pan—besides building two monumental *pláts* on that board—and prepare a cold *entrée*. But he cheerfully set to work to overcome difficulties, achieved his task, and was rewarded by the plaudits of the diners. Such difficulties as these our servants never have to encounter, and a cheerful endeavor to make the best of everything should be the rule. Yet, let us spare them all the labor we can, or rather make it as easy and pleasant as possible; they will be more proud of their well-furnished kitchen, more cheerful in it, than they will of one where everything for their convenience is grudged, and such pride and cheerfulness will be your gain.

There is always a great deal of talk about servants in America, how bad and inefficient they are, how badly they contrast with those of England. Certainly, they

Chapter of Odds and Ends—Valedictory.

are not so efficient as those of the older country; how could they be? There, girls who are intended for servants have ever held before their eyes what they may or may not do in the future calling, and how it is to be done. But take one of these orderly, efficient girls, put her in an American family as general servant or as cook, where two are kept, washing and ironing to do, and a variety of other work, and see how your English servant would stare at your requirements. She has been accustomed to her own line of work at home; if housemaid, she has been dressed for the day at noon; if cook, she has never done even her own washing.

She may, and will no doubt, fall into the way of the country, after a while, and on account of her early habits of respect, will make a good servant perhaps. But many of them would be quite indignant at being asked to do the average servant's work here. I am speaking now of the *trained* servants; but, comparing the London "maid-of-all-work" or "slavey" with our own general servants, and considering how much more is expected of the latter, the comparison seems to me vastly in the favor of our own Bridgets. We may rest assured, however smoothly the wheels of household management glide along in wealthy families across the water, people who can only keep one or two have all our troubles with servants and a few added, and their faults are just as general a subject of conversation among ladies.

France (out of Paris, from Parisian servants deliver me!) and Germany seem the favored lands where one servant does the work of three or four. Yet even they, are, they say, degenerating. Let us, then, be contented and make the best of what we have, assured that even Biddy is not so hopeless as she is painted. Kindness (not weakness), firmness, and patience work wonders, even with the roughest Emerald that ever crossed the sea.

I have said somewhere else that you must beware of attempting too much at once; perfect yourself in one thing before you attempt another. Take breaded chops or fried oysters, make opportunities for having them rather often, and do not rest satisfied until you have them as well fried as you have ever seen them anywhere; "practice makes perfect," and you certainly will achieve perfection if you are not discouraged by one failure. But above all things never make experiments for company; let them be made when it really matters little whether you succeed or not, and let your experiments be on a *small* scale; don't attempt to fry a *large* dish of oysters or chops until it is a very easy task, or make more than half a pound of puff paste at first; for if you fail with a large task before you, you will be tired and disheartened, hate the sight of what you are doing, and, as a consequence, not be likely to return to it very soon. The same may be said of cooks; some of them are very fond of experiments, which taste I should always encourage; but do not let them jump from one experiment to the other; if they try a dish and fail, they often make up their minds that the fault is not theirs, that it is not worth while to "bother" with it. Here your knowledge will be of service; you will show them that it can be done, how it should be done, and order the dish cook failed in, frequently, giving it sufficient surveillance to prevent your family suffering from her inexperience; for, as a witty Frenchman said of Mme. du Deffaud's cook, "Between her and Brinvilliers there is only the difference of intention."

Few things add more to a man or woman's social reputation than the fact that they keep a good table. It need not be one where

> "The strong table groans
> Beneath the smoking sirloin stretched immense;"

but a table where whatever you do have will be good, be it pork and beans, or salmi; the pork and beans would satisfy a Bostonian, the salmi Grimod de la Reynière himself. I do not admit with Di Walcott that

> "The turnpike road to people's hearts I find
> Lies through their mouths, or I mistake mankind."

But it is a fact that good living—by this I do not mean extravagant living—presupposes good breeding. Well-bred people sometimes live badly; but ill-bred people seldom or ever live well, in the right sense of the term.

Now, by way of valedictory, let me repeat that I do not think a lady's best or proper place is the kitchen; but it is quite possible to have a perfectly served table, yet spend very little time there. Only that one little hour a day that Talleyrand, the busy man full of intrigue and statecraft, found time to spend with his cook, would insure your table being well served. For, after devoting say a few winter months to perfecting yourself in a few things, you will be able to teach your cook, who is often ambitious to excel if put in the right way. A word here about cooks.

The knowledge that if they fail to do a thing well you will do it yourself, will often put them on their mettle to do their best; while the feeling that you don't know, will make them careless.

Servants have a great deal more *amour propre* than people imagine; therefore, stimulate it by judicious praise and appreciation; let them think that to send in a dish perfect, is a glory to themselves as well as a pleasure to you. While careful to remark when alone with them upon any fault that results from carelessness, be equally careful to give all the praise you can, and repeat to them complimentary remarks that may have been made on their skill. Servants are usually—such is the weakness of feminine nature, whether in the drawing-room or the kitchen—very sensitive to the praise or blame of the gentlemen of the family. Indulge poor humanity a little when you honestly can.

INDEX.

	PAGE
Almond creams	93
Altering recipes	111, 112
Asparagus, to boil	66
Baba	86
Small	87
Syrup for	87
Batter for frying à la Carême	59
" " " Provençale	60
Beef, Bœuf à la jardinière	74
" au Gratin	75
Filet de bœuf Chateaubriand	49
Fritadella	81
Little breakfast dish of	78
Miroton of	76
Olives of	79
Pseudo-beefsteak	75
Ragout of cold	78
Salmi of cold	73
Simplest way to warm a joint	77
To warm over a large piece	73
Sirloin, to make two dishes	49
Biscuit glacé, à la Charles Dickens	85
" " Thackeray	85
Blanc for white sauce	31
Boiling, asparagus	66
Cabbage	65
Potatoes	66
Peas	65
Rules for meat	65
Bouchées de dames	88
To ice	89
Bread	12
Baking	14
Cause of failure	15
" of thick crust	14
Compressed yeast	15
Kneading	14
Oven heating	14
Remarks	12
Rules of time for rising	14
To set sponge	13
Bread-crumbs for frying	56
Bread dough, to keep a day or two	106
" for pie crust	97
Soufflée	20
Brioche	18
Jockey Club, recipe for	19

	PAGE
Brioche for summer pastry	19, 20
Broiling	60
Chickens and birds	61
Brown flour	34
Sauce	71
Butter, maître d'hôtel	32
Montpellier	33
Ravigotte	33
Cabbage, to boil	65
Cakes, Baba	86
Bouchées de dames	88
Savarins	88
Candies	92
Chocolate creams	94
Cream almonds	93
Cream walnuts	93
Fondant	92
Fondant panaché	93
Punch drops	94
Simple French	92
Tutti frutti	92
Vanilla almond cream	92
Walnut cream	92
Celeriac, or turnip-rooted celery	54
Celery seed for soup	106
Celery cream soup	84
Chateaubriand, filet de bœuf	49
Chicken	48
Broiling	60
Cold	49
Pie	38
Potted	44
Roasting	48
Use of the feet	48
Clinkered fire-bricks	107
Cold meat salmi	73
Various ways of warming	72–81
Coloring for candy and icing	95
Company to lunch, and nothing in the house	44
Cromesquis of cold lamb	75
Crumbs for frying	56
Cucumber and onion ragout	102
Curaçoa, to make	89
Curry	106
Deviled meats	80
Dishes made without meat	102

	PAGE
Dripping, to clarify	59
Feuilletonage	23
Fire-bricks, to remove clinkers from	107
To mend	107
Flavoring	70
Flounders, to bone	56
As filet de sole	56
Forequarter of mutton	101
Frangipane tartlets	26
French herbs	113
Friandises	84
Fritadella of cold meat, twenty recipes in one	81
Frying	55
Butter à la Carême	59
" Provençale	60
Crumbing	56
Filet de sole	56
Flounders	56
Oil for	58
Oysters	57
Remarks on	55
To clarify dripping for	59
To test the heat of fat for	57
Galantine	39
Garlic	108
Glaze	30
To glaze ham, tongue, etc	32
Gouffé's pot-au-feu	68
Rules for ovens	27
Gravy	29-63
Grating nutmegs	105
Ham, to boil	65
To glaze	32
To pot	43
Hash	97
Heart, beef	100
Sheep's	99
Iced soufflée	85
A la Byron	84
Icing	89
Ink, to remove from carpets	107
Jellied fish or oysters	41
Jelly for cold chicken	47
Jelly from pork	31
Kerosene lamps	107
Keeping meat	106
Poultry	107
Dough	106
Kitchen conveniences	114
Kreuznach horns	16
Kringles	17
Lamb, cromesquis of	75
Lamps	107
Larding needle	112
Leg of mutton	52
A la Soubise	52
Boiled	52
Lemons, to keep	105
Peels	106
Little dinners	50
Liver, sheep's	98
Luncheons	35
Maître d'hôtel butter	32

	PAGE
Management in small families	47
Maraschino, to make	90
Marrow from soup bone	98
Mayonnaise, new	42
Meat, to keep	106
Salad	52
Mephistophelian sauce	81
Miroton of beef	76
Montpellier butter	33
Mushroom powder	29
Mutton broth	52
Forequarter	101
Leg	52
Neck of mutton	101
Noyeau	90
Nutmegs, best way to grate	105
Omelet, new	45
Onion soup, maigre	103
Ornamenting meat pies	37
Ovens	14
Gouffé's rules for heating	27
Oysters, to fry	57
In jelly	41
Ox cheek	100
Panaché fondant	93
Parsley seed for soup	106
Parsley in winter	113
Paste, puff	22
To handle	24
Pastry tablets	26
Pâte à la Carême for frying	59
" Provençale	60
Peas, to boil	66
Pease soup, maigre	103
Pie, bread dough for crust	97
Chicken, to eat cold	38
Fruit	24
English raised	38
To " raise " a	39
Veal and ham	38
Windsor	36
Pork for jelly	31
Potato salad	54
Snow	45
Soup, maigre	103
To warm over	46
Pot-au-feu	68
Pot roasts	99
Potted meats	43
Punch drops	94
Ragout of cold meat	78
Of cucumber and onion	102
Ravigotte	33
Remarks, preliminary	1-12
On boiling	65
On bread-making	12
On frying	54
On kitchen and servants	114
On little dinners	50
On luncheons	35
On maigre dishes	104
On management in small families	47
On sauces and flavoring	70

Index.

	PAGE		PAGE
Remarks on soups	67	Soup bone	96
On table prejudices	108	Soup, celery cream	68
On true economy in buying meat	99	Consommé	68
On roasting	62	Pot-au-feu	68
Rissolettes	25	Onion	103
Rolls	15	Pease	103
Roux	34	Potato	103
Rusks	16	To color	67
Salad, Celeraic	54	To clear stock	66
Potato	54	Sugar boiling for candy	91
Cold meat	52	Tainted meat, to restore	107
Salamander, substitute for	112	To make strong vegetables milder	106
Sauces	70	Tutti frutti candy	92
Flavoring	70	Vanilla almond cream	92
Brown or espagnole	71	Veal	53
Mephistophelian	81	Warming over	72
White	71	What to do with scraps	45
Mayonnaise	42	Where to buy articles not in general use	112
Savarin (cake)	88		
Soufflée bread	20	Why meat does not brown in cooking	62
Iced	85		
A la Byron	84	Windsor pie	36

www.ingramcontent.com/pod-product-compliance
Lightning Source LLC
Chambersburg PA
CBHW020107170426
43199CB00009B/438